Not weeded
BCL 3
1-05 BHS

BY THE SAME AUTHOR

Plato's Later Epistemology

With PETER LASLETT (ed.)
Philosophy, Politics and Society
Second Series

SOCIAL SCIENCE AND
POLITICAL THEORY

SOCIAL SCIENCE AND POLITICAL THEORY

BY

W. G. RUNCIMAN

Fellow of Trinity College, Cambridge

CAMBRIDGE
AT THE UNIVERSITY PRESS
1963

PUBLISHED BY
THE SYNDICS OF THE CAMBRIDGE UNIVERSITY PRESS

Bentley House, 200 Euston Road, London, N.W. 1
American Branch: 32 East 57th Street, New York 22, N.Y.
West African Office: P.O. Box 33, Ibadan, Nigeria

©

CAMBRIDGE UNIVERSITY PRESS

1963

Printed in Great Britain at the University Press, Cambridge
(Brooke Crutchley, University Printer)

CONTENTS

Preface		*page* vii
I	The Nature of Social Science	1
II	The Emergence of Political Sociology	22
III	Karl Marx and Max Weber	43
IV	Élites and Oligarchies	64
V	Voters and Parties	87
VI	Methods, Models and Theories	109
VII	Class, Status and Political Conflict	135
VIII	Social Science and Political Theory	156
Notes		176
Index		198

PREFACE

These essays are based on a course of lectures delivered in Cambridge during the autumn of 1961 and broadcast in a shortened form in the B.B.C. Third Programme in the spring of 1962. I have more or less retained their original form, but I have added a number of notes which will be found collected together at the end of the volume. These are designed both to give references where this seems necessary and also to follow up some of the arguments in more detail than the non-specialist reader would wish to find in the text. Where reference is made to works in a foreign language, I have normally used English versions where available; I have, however, sometimes altered the translation without acknowledgement.

My thanks are due to the following, who read earlier drafts of one or more chapters and gave me the benefit of their comments: Professor Reinhard Bendix, Professor Sir Isaiah Berlin, Mr Robert Cassen, Mr Peter Laslett, Dr David Lockwood and Professor Edward Shils. Chapter VIII owes much to a discussion with Mr Renford Bambrough. For the errors of fact and emphasis which remain I alone am responsible. I am inevitably aware, in a book of this kind, of touching superficially on a diversity of topics all of which are better known to many others than to myself. My only defence is the hope that it may help to show over how wide a range of issues the sociology and philosophy of politics necessarily involve each other.

W. G. R.

TRINITY COLLEGE, CAMBRIDGE
July 1962

CHAPTER I

THE NATURE OF SOCIAL SCIENCE

If sociology is defined as the systematic study of collective human behaviour, then such separate disciplines as economics, or demography, or criminology, or politics should be regarded as co-ordinate but distinctive branches of sociology (or social science). By such a definition, the contrast sometimes drawn between economics and sociology is clearly a false one. Economic behaviour, like political behaviour, is one kind of social behaviour, and economic or political institutions are one kind of social institution; and if there were such a thing as a general social theory (which I do not believe there is), it would have to include the theories of both economics and politics under it.[1] In fact, the unqualified term 'sociology' usually turns out on inspection to mean one or more of three very different things: first, contemporary social history or anthropology;[2] second, collective or social psychology; and third—when it is at its most general level—the sort of speculation about the total historical process which should more properly be bracketed with the philosophy of history.

If, however, there could be such a thing as a general social theory, we should at least be clear at the outset what it would look like. Briefly, we may say that it would consist of a set of general, testable, explanatory propositions applicable to the total area of collective human behaviour. This may not seem to be saying very much; but it serves to make clear the crucial distinction between classification and analysis—that is, between saying what something is and saying how it works—which has been sadly disregarded by some very prolific but cloudy-minded sociological theorists. This distinction applies equally to those particular social sciences where the search for general explanatory statements is likely to be more rewarding. In addition, there is the different distinction between—in the case of politics—political philosophy or political theory and political sociology or political science. Though these two latter terms are sometimes differentiated,[1] they may be treated as synonymous in terms of the basic distinction between the philosophical and the empirical study of politics. Although, as we shall see, this is not so absolute a distinction as has sometimes been supposed, it is still a significant and useful one: a theory of political sociology will be a proposition of 'if...then' form analogous, at least, to the theories of natural science; the propositions of political theory or philosophy will, by contrast, be in some sense prescriptive or ethical statements (except where they are purely logical).[2]

There have, of course, been numerous general theories of history or society whose authors have claimed for them the validity of science; nor am I arguing that there could never be some general psychological laws from which the explanation of collective human behaviour might be derived.[3] The fact is, however, that what have been claimed as sciences of society have never turned out to be more than philosophies of history. This applies not only to the various eighteenth-century attempts to found sciences of morals and history, but likewise (and not least) to Marxism, despite the claim made by Engels at Marx's graveside that 'just as Darwin discovered the law of development of organic nature, so Marx discovered the law of development of human history'.[4] A more recent alternative candidate to

The Nature of Social Science

Marxism has been the so-called 'functionalist' approach taken over from biology by the social anthropologists (to which I shall come back in chapter VI). Its claim may, at first glance, be reinforced by the argument that since anthropologists have given us descriptions of what now amount to hundreds of total societies it should be possible to derive from their observations some sort of law or laws about total societies as such. Any such conclusion, however, would be foolhardy. Not only has no such law been successfully put forward, but damaging logical criticisms have been brought against the functionalist approach. Moreover, it would be a mistake to suppose that anthropologists, even when dealing with relatively small and simple societies, are giving us a total description. It may be that they are asking the very general question 'What is life like in Middletown?' (or Tepoztlan or Cornerville or wherever it may be). It may also be true that it is impossible to describe, let alone to explain, any one aspect of a society's life in isolation. Nevertheless, the social scientist who asks 'What is life like among the so-and-so?' may be rather like a natural scientist getting off a train at Brighton and asking 'What is matter like in Sussex?'. A theory of kinship, or prices, or industrial relations, or birth-rates, or criminal behaviour, may be a possible or at least not inconceivable goal. But to start by looking for a general theory of society is likely to remain—as it has so far proved to be—a waste of effort.

This is not to deny that there is a great deal both in vocabulary and in method which is shared between the various areas of social science.[1] Furthermore, it is obvious that the various areas depend at many points on one another for their substantive conclusions. But to wish to lump them all together under a single explanatory heading is to adopt a kind of pre-Socratic approach. Only in the very early days of natural science was it reasonable or interesting to suggest, like Thales of Ionia, that everything is water; and only in the very early days of systematic social science was it reasonable or interesting to suggest, like Marx and Engels, that every social act, institution or relation is basically economic. What we might call the extreme pre-Socratic assumption is in fact explicitly made not only by Marx but also by the coiner of the term 'sociology', Auguste Comte. Marx wrote in his *Economic and Philosophical Manuscripts of 1844* that 'natural science will in time incorporate the science of man, just as the science of man will incorporate natural science: there will be one science',[1] and Comte, in a piece of typically rhetorical bombast in the *Politique Positive*, declared that 'this creation of social science, by completing the upward flight of our contemplations of reality, impresses upon them the systematic character which they still lacked by providing them with the sole universal link of which they admit'.[2] It is hard to suppose, however, that there is nowadays anyone who would take either of these grandiose claims very seriously.

There is, indeed, a strong case for abandoning altogether the use of 'sociology' as an unqualified term, and referring always to industrial sociology or the sociology of law or religion or whatever it might be. Descriptive sociology would then be described as social history or anthropology; general theorizing about total societies would, as I have already suggested, be bracketed with the philosophy of history; and social psychology (experimental or otherwise) would be referred to specifically as such. If nothing else, the emphasis on the specialized nature of the different branches of social science should make clear the absurdity of the dispute which goes on about quantitative versus non-

The Nature of Social Science

quantitative sociology. A great number of problems in the social sciences quite obviously require quantitative methods for their solution: an economist estimating national incomes or a demographer predicting differential fertility rates can hardly do useful work without the help of numbers. But equally, there are a great variety of problems where quantitative methods would be quite out of place: a comparative assessment of the motives and influence of Robespierre and Lenin will not be best attempted by equations. Nor is it the case that where quantitative methods are appropriate the results achieved are necessarily more 'scientific' than where they are not: the single example of Darwin is quite enough to dispose of any such view. Each particular sort of problem will have an appropriate set of techniques with which to approach it, and even within a particular branch of social science (as we shall see with politics) some problems are as suitable for quantitative treatment as others are not.

It may, therefore, be almost as misleading to talk without qualification about 'sociological methods' as about 'sociology'. To talk of social science only becomes relevant when a particular area of human behaviour is isolated and a theory (or model) of a general 'if...then' form is put forward to explain it. There is only one fundamental question which should be asked at the level of social science or sociology in general and which must precede any concrete discussion of a particular area of social science. Given that the subject matter of all the social sciences is not things but people, is it possible to talk of 'science' at all in the sense in which the term is normally used?

This is not only a large question, but an overworked one. It involves not only the logical and epistemological problems of social science method, but also the vexed and complex topics disputed among philosophers of history. But despite the enormous amounts that have been written on all this, there are only two fundamental disputes which are directly relevant to the argument of these essays. I do not suggest for a moment that they are disputes which can be definitively resolved. I do, however, wish to suggest that they can best be circumvented by proceeding on lines laid down by Max Weber.

The first dispute is between the individualists on one side and the holists on the other. There are several variants of both these positions, but the central question is the ontological status of the objects of social science. It is, self-evidently, a philosophical question: when we speak of a social group, or a nation-state, or an economy, or a political system, what exactly do we mean? In practice, the answer is often unimportant. The best procedure is probably to follow the cyberneticists and to treat all collectivities as systems, such systems being operationally defined not as things but as sets of variables.[1] But the question itself is not at all easy to answer. It has exercised a good many philosophers as such, and there does not seem to be any firm agreement among them as to just what we mean when we make such statements as 'Germany invaded France'. The individualists maintain that any statement about a collectivity must be in principle reducible to a set of statements about the individuals of whom the collectivity is composed. But the holists argue that in order to talk about—to give one of their favourite examples—a banking system[2] we need to introduce concepts which depend for their meaning precisely on the fact that they can never be reduced to a list of assertions about individuals. Most of the disputants (apart, that is, from those who want to make extravagant statements about the 'group mind' or the 'organic state' or the 'collective unconscious') would probably agree that it is a mistake

The Nature of Social Science

to speak of collectivities as having such things as ideas and purposes which can only be properly predicated of individual people. But beyond this, the argument does not seem likely to be resolved to the satisfaction of both parties.

I do not think, however, that this need worry us very much. It will obviously be annoying for the social scientist to be told by a philosopher that the subject of the proposition he is trying to establish is merely a sort of pretended reference which does not in fact denote anything at all. But what matters is that we should know how to test any proposition about a collectivity. If we can show to the sceptical philosopher how a given proposition could be validated (or at any rate falsified), then it can be safely treated as meaningful. It is here that it will be convenient if we can define the collectivity in terms of a set of variables; but even without this, what matters is to know how the proposition could be falsified. This need not require us to deny, dogmatically, any meaning whatever to such terms as Troeltsch's 'concrete individual wholes' or Durkheim's 'collective consciousness'. It merely means that we should use them as terms in the propositions of social science only when their empirical falsifiability is clear.

When, therefore, we attach predicates to such terms we must be able to specify the observable action involved. This is where Weber's viewpoint is useful. Weber is emphatic that what we are talking about when we say that a collectivity exists is a 'probability of action' appropriate in a specified way to the meaning attached to the collectivity. This does not mean that for some purposes (for instance, juristic) it may not be necessary to treat a business corporation or a state as if it were a person. It does mean, however, that when a sociologist formulates a proposition about such a collectivity he must be able to specify the concrete social action which the proposition denotes. By this means, we can not only see how a given proposition might in principle, at least, be falsified, but we can also avoid treating a collectivity as if it were a tangible object—the 'fallacy of reification' which incenses the individualists. As to whether the account of social action involves concepts which are irreducible according to the canons of 'methodological individualism', we are not required to commit ourselves.

The second dispute, however, in which the two sides are the positivists and the intuitionists, is more complicated and also more important. The positivists are those who in general regard the social sciences (under which they may well include history) as methodologically equivalent to the natural sciences; that is to say, they regard the differences between the two as being of a purely technical kind. The intuitionists strongly reject this claim, but they do so on one or both of two main grounds which need to be carefully distinguished. The first is that every historical event is unique in a way that the experiments or replications of natural science are not: an experiment can always be repeated, but never a segment of history. The second ground (which is, however, not entirely unrelated to the first) is that human behaviour has meaning to the agents performing it. As one of the most celebrated intuitionists put it, 'Geology presents us with a series of *events*, but history is not history unless it presents us with a series of *acts*'.[1] Weber's position, as I understand it on this topic, is that both sides are partly right and partly wrong; but Weber, like Marx, is one of those authors who tends to have as many interpretations as readers, and he has on occasion been claimed as an ally or denounced as a heretic by both sides. What I shall try briefly to do is to suggest

The Nature of Social Science

that his demonstration that both and neither are right reveals the argument to be in large part factitious.

Let us first of all take the 'uniqueness' argument. There is, of course, a sense going back to Heraclitus in which every event is unique. But the point at issue here is obviously more than this. The objects or events with which the natural scientist repeats his experiments or accumulates his examples can be treated as equivalent with each other. But no other person can be regarded as interchangeable with Napoleon: the events of which his actions and intentions were a part, and which the historian wishes causally to explain, are wholly and intrinsically impossible to replicate. From this, the intuitionist argument holds that generalization is bound to be irrelevant: if the particular event has not been explained, it cannot be incorporated into a generalization, whereas if it has been explained, the generalization is unnecessary to explain it. The positivists, however, have two lines of answer to this. The first and most extreme is Engels's notion of 'substitute Napoleons', according to which Napoleon's most personal characteristics are all the determined outcome of economic laws. On this view, the iron laws of history make the actions (and their results) of any Napoleon inevitably what they are; if this particular Napoleon had not happened, so the argument runs, the underlying impersonal forces would have come up with another one. The second and less radical answer is to reject the substitution of Napoleons but to argue that every person and his actions, though neither interchangeable nor replicable, can still be explained only by general 'scientific' laws of human behaviour. Neither answer, however, will adequately withstand objection. Plekhanov, of all the Marxists, made the most interesting attempt to modify the extreme determinism of Engels by allowing for the exceptional man who may, so to speak, surpass his allotted historical role. But as Weber at one point graphically observes, the materialist conception of history is not a cab one can get off and on at will—once on, one has to stay for the ride. The less extreme positivistic position, which concedes validity to individual characters and intentions but claims that they are reducible in terms of general laws of human behaviour, can be countered simply by pointing out that no such reduction has been successfully made. Different people will respond differently to different situations in the light of knowledge which is now unforeseeable, and any procedure on the strict model of natural science is therefore bound to break down.

Although, however, we must concede to the intuitionists that every historical event is unique and that this difference is crucial, we are not thereby driven defenceless into the heart of the intuitionist camp. For it is also true that all historical explanations depend at some point on the notion of 'what would have happened if...?', and this in turn does derive its validity from some general notions of cause. Without these, historians would be deprived of the use of even such words as 'dangerous'; and unless it is literally nonsense—which not even the most extreme intuitionists maintain—to assign proportional causal weights in any given (unique) historical sequence, then general explanations must have in principle some validity. Any explanation, indeed, has implicit reference to a general law. No serious historian gives only a single reason in answer to the question why a particular event occurred. He gives instead a list of causes (or of necessary and sufficient conditions) whose relative importance it is his business to assign. His interpretation will depend on generalized or 'nomothetic' assumptions about historical cause and effect which could not

The Nature of Social Science

possibly be solely deduced from the particular sequence he wishes to explain. It therefore follows that both intuitionists and positivists are partly right, but neither is altogether as right as they have been apt to claim. Every historical sequence is unique, but this does not deny validity to general causal explanations. General causal explanations have validity; but history is not reducible entirely to determinate instances of fully articulated sets of such laws. The historian (and therefore the social scientist) can never be a thoroughgoing positivist; but he must, once he has realized this, still try to behave up to a point as though he were.

The second major intuitionist argument, which derives from the assertion that human behaviour is (unlike that of the objects of natural science) meaningful, raises some of the most far-reaching philosophical issues of all. But without entering into the logical complexities of motives and intentions, we may initially follow Weber in regarding social behaviour as meaningful by definition. According to Weber, 'action' covers all behaviour to which a subjective meaning is attached by the agent, and social action covers all action which takes account of the behaviour of others by virtue of the subjective meaning attached to it by the agent.[1] This excludes, for instance, lunacy of certain kinds. But although such behaviour may require explanation just as much as any other, the social scientist is not as such concerned with it once it ceases to fulfil Weber's definition. The crucial question for our present topic is how far the meaningfulness of social action makes a social science impossible. It is here that we must introduce Weber's famous notion of 'understanding' (*Verstehen*).

It would obviously be absurd to claim to have explained a sequence of social behaviour without having any idea of what it means to the participants. This will apply, moreover, even if our observation of successive uniformities enables us to make verified predictions about the course of this behaviour. If, for example, an observer watches a group of people who under certain circumstances exchange small pieces of paper and metal, after which one of them gives another an object which the recipient then takes away, he may in due course be able to make accurate predictions about the transfer of goods in this community by correlating such transfers with the exchange of metal pieces. But unless he has grasped the ideas of money, buying and selling, and so on, we shall deny his claim to have explained what is going on. This sort of illustration appears at first sight to force us back among the intuitionists again; and indeed, some interpreters of Weber have taken his sense of *Verstehen* to entail an intuitionist position. But this is not so. Weber is emphatic that even the most self-evident interpretation requires to be validated—Weber, indeed, is prepared to use the word 'verified'—by reference to concrete empirical evidence. 'Verification of subjective interpretation,' he says, 'by comparison with the concrete course of events is, as in the case of all hypotheses, indispensable';[1] and, as a successful example of this procedure, he cites Gresham's law.

There are, of course, more problems raised than this by the notion of 'understanding' the behaviour of others. It may at the outset be prudent to treat such generalizations as Gresham's law as more provisional than Weber suggests. Moreover, quite apart from the question of what constitutes empirical verification, the notion of understanding is itself highly complex. Can we claim, for instance, to have understood another person's behaviour if the person himself disagrees with the interpretation offered? This is a problem most notoriously raised by Freudian explanations of

The Nature of Social Science

behaviour, which often presuppose that the analyst can understand the patient's behaviour better than the patient has yet been brought to realize. Similarly, how far is the observer of an alien culture justified in imposing a terminology which the members of that culture will not accept as adequate to explain their customs or practices? These are very difficult questions, of which several variants or aspects will recur throughout these essays; nor are they questions to which Weber or anyone else has succeeded in propounding a definitive solution. As we shall see, however, they are ultimately philosophical questions, and this is all that for the moment I want to emphasize. What Weber's discussion makes clear is that some form both of 'internal' comprehension and of 'external' confirmation are necessary to justify any sociological explanation. We see once again that we must try to behave as though we could be positivists, but that this is on condition that we realize that positivistic procedures must be supplemented (or preceded) by a further procedure which is different in kind.

I have done no more than sketch the outlines of what I believe to be the two major issues, but I hope I have said enough to show how Weber's general thesis makes possible the circumvention, if not the resolution, of both. The situation is, however, sometimes further complicated by the incursions on to the field of battle of disputants whose affiliation is not quite to either of the schools which can be broadly labelled intuitionists and positivists. Professor Karl Popper is perhaps the best known of these. Popper is not only opposed to intuitionism, which he wishes to assimilate by force to the hypothetical method of natural science; he is also opposed to positivism, in that his fiercest onslaughts are directed against any attempt to construct a predictive science of history. This is not as inconsistent as it might appear, for his objection to what he calls—in a special and sometimes inconsistent use of the term—'historicism' is on technical grounds which need not always conflict with his wish to equate the 'understanding' involved in both natural and social science. Moreover, much of his objection to 'historicism' (in his sense) derives from his position on the individualist/holist dispute, for Popper is the founding father of the so-called 'methodological individualists'. His approach to the intuitionist issue, however, begs just that question to which I believe Weber to be offering an answer.

Weber does get some mild credit from Popper for seeing that intuitive understanding must always be controlled by ordinary scientific canons and methods.[1] But in at the same time criticizing Weber for being an intuitionist, he disregards Weber's essential point. Despite the need for scientific controls wherever possible, the meaningful nature of social behaviour requires that it should be explained in terms additional to those adequate for the natural sciences. Furthermore, the meaningful nature of human action is in fact a necessary presupposition of some of Popper's own arguments against 'historicism'. Several further issues at this point cut across what is already an intricate argument, and I do not wish to attempt a criticism of Popper's analysis of historical explanation (where, incidentally, he does again give some credit to Weber).[2] All I am saying is that Popper's position on intuitionism by-passes the sense in which understanding is an obvious prerequisite of sociological explanation. The point is not that sociologists, of whatever kind, are failing to achieve their goal of a science in the single sense that Popper allows science to have. The point is rather that a science in Popper's sense of science should not be their goal at all.

In practice, the most important problem which follows from the nature of the social sciences is one which can be very simply put and which Weber at many points comes back to: choice of words. It follows directly from the notion of 'understanding', some of the difficulties of which I have already hinted at. It is not, of course, a problem which necessarily arises every time we formulate a proposition in the social sciences. Terms, for instance, like 'price' or 'vote' raise few, if any, difficulties. Even terms like 'crime' and 'responsibility' can sometimes be treated positivistically, for they can be understood simply by reference to the provisions of an existing legal system. The difficulty comes when the explanation of a social practice or event depends on specifying of what it is an instance—when, for example, we offer as an explanation (not merely a description) of a tribal ritual the suggestion that it is not 'magical' but 'religious'. It is not simply a question of definitions, for all definitions, after all, can be regarded as arbitrary. The problem lies rather in the presuppositions which must underlie the choice of vocabulary in which an explanation is to be given. The fact that our formulation of the 'why?' question and its answer yield us a series of confirmed predictions is not, as we have already seen, enough. We must in addition, if we are to claim to give a proper explanation, be sure that we are using the 'right' or 'appropriate' terms.

Weber persistently and correctly emphasizes that there can be no definitive vocabulary for the analysis of social phenomena. Even the concept of 'culture' is a value-concept. The construction of the conceptual scheme to be used in a sociological inquiry depends, says Weber, on the fundamental point of view (*Gesichtspunkt*), on the evaluative notions (*Wertideen*) of the investigator and his age. There are no positivistic criteria on which the choice can be made. Precisely this point has been much more recently made by Professor Hampshire in his philosophical essay *Thought and Action*. In speaking of mental as opposed to physical concepts, Hampshire says that 'any philosopher has to make a choice of a set of explanatory terms which bring out the distinctions, already present in common speech, that he particularly wants to stress. At this point, he unavoidably enters the domain of morality.'[1] What this means, in the context of these present essays, is that a political sociology—that is, an explanation or set of explanations of political behaviour—must depend even for its vocabulary on some kind of philosophical position. This derives directly from the fact that the social sciences deal with actions and not events. It does not, as we have seen, require us to abandon all notions of following scientific method in sociological inquiry. What it does is to impose a limit on the validity of positivistic methods; these must supplement, but can never replace, a further procedure of inquiry which is fundamentally different in kind.

There are, of course, a number of other objections which have been raised in denial of the possibility of social science, apart from the two disputes of which I have tried to give a résumé. These, however, are of a less fundamental character and can be treated (as by the positivists) as technical. It is denied, for instance, that we can ever generalize about human affairs, because of the impossibility of conducting historical experiments. But this is equally true of astronomy or geology, and these two branches of learning are not normally denied a claim to science. It is true that historical sequences are unique in a further and different sense which does not apply to the movement of planets or the shrinkage of the crust of the earth; the latter are cases of events which can be treated as equivalent to others, and can be explained by reference to some sets of general laws. But, as we have seen, this does not deny to the social scientist the right to try to generalize; it merely means that his generalizations are on a different basis. Similarly, it is sometimes said of social science that it involves too many variables to make scientific procedure possible; this is a worry voiced even from within the positivistic camp, and can, for instance, be found in both Herbert Spencer and J. S. Mill. But this is equally true of meteorology, which is surely no less a science (even though a less successful one) than the others. The reason that social science is not analogous to meteorology is rather that any prediction made by a social scientist is about people who can by their conscious action upset the prediction made.[1] The proper function of a social science, on the analysis I have tried to give, is not prediction but diagnosis.

Suppose a doctor, after a thorough examination, tells a heart patient that if he is careful he should have at least five more years to live. The diagnosis will not be falsified if, on the following morning, the patient runs up six flights of stairs and then drops dead at the top. In the same way, a political sociologist (or historian) may say that a given country will under certain conditions go Communist or, less ambitiously, that a given party will under certain conditions win the next election. But he cannot pretend to predict the unique historical occurrences and individual intentions which will have an effect on the diagnosis provisionally given. The 'logical refutation' of historicism which Professor Popper outlines in the preface to his *Poverty of Historicism* is, if not yet a formal proof, still effective enough: we cannot know what will only be known by the subjects of our predictions, and will alter their behaviour accordingly. But this does not (as, indeed, Popper explicitly concedes) destroy the validity of general propositions about social phenomena of an 'if...then' form. Of the various social sciences, it is economics which has most successfully put forward such propositions—a success due, reputedly, to the usefulness of assuming 'rational' pursuit of profit, as well as to the appropriateness for the subject-matter of quantitative techniques. But this is a technical advantage, not a difference in logical kind. There is in principle no reason why analogous propositions or theories should not be put forward by demographers, or theorists of kinship, or criminologists, or political scientists.

We are still left, however, with the commonest and most tiresome type of objection which is liable to be levelled against social science. The social sciences are all concerned with people, and people are apt—quite naturally—to have ideas of their own about how and why they and other people in general behave. They have thus a standard rejoinder with which they can confront any proposition advanced by a sociologist: if they agree with it, it is obvious; if they disagree with it, it is wrong. Much the best answer that I know of to this sort of attitude is that given by Professor Lazarsfeld of Columbia University (whose work I shall be returning to at several later points in these essays). In a review of *The American Soldier*, the monumental social-psychological study of the American army which was carried out during the Second World War, Lazarsfeld lists a number of conclusions which, he says, most people would probably dismiss as obvious.[1] He lists six such obvious propositions: for instance, that better-educated men showed more psycho-neurotic symptoms during training, that Southerners stood up better to tropical climate than Northerners, and that white private soldiers were more eager for promotion than Negroes. All these conclusions could have been directly deduced from current platitudes about neurotic intellectuals, unambitious Negroes, and so on. But the interesting thing, as Lazarsfeld points out, about all these obvious conclusions is that they are false. Moreover, whichever of two contradictory (but, of course, obvious) propositions of this kind is found on systematic inquiry to be correct, there will always be somebody to maintain that he knew it all beforehand. What the social scientist has to do is to establish which of two contradictory truisms is correct, and to what extent and under what conditions it holds good. The only way to do this is to follow as far as possible, given the necessary reservations I have been discussing, the procedures of scientific method.

This leaves, finally, only the most general and speculative question: how far is social science likely to progress? To try too hard to offer an answer to this is not only a difficult undertaking but a foolish one, for anyone who knew would, as it were, be there already. Nobody has yet successfully produced a general theory of societies, and it is hard not to doubt whether anybody ever will. But it is just as rash to venture opinions about where knowledge cannot go as where it can; and it is salutary to remember that when Boyle of Boyle's law was working on gases, plenty of people were ready to tell him on good *a priori* grounds that he was wasting his time: how, after all, can one possibly weigh air? Universities are full of academic subjects which began as philosophy but have ended up as science. I have been agreeing with those who maintain that positivistic claims for the social sciences are *a priori* wrong because of two crucial features which distinguish the natural sciences from the social. But the history of science is cluttered with the corpses of arguments of just this kind. The only safe prediction to make about a branch of knowledge is that it is bound to change one way or the other, and probably in a direction that few of its practitioners at a given time would suspect.

Nevertheless, one tentative guess is perhaps worth venturing. A significant advance has still to be made in the social sciences in the large, uncertain and difficult area where psychological factors interact or overlap with social. When our subject-matter is people, their collective behaviour has to be explained by reference to factors both inside and outside of them: when, that is to say, we are explaining the kinship structure of Trobrianders or the voting behaviour of Poujadists, we need not only to understand the social forces acting on them (institutions, parties, economic conditions and so on) but also the psychological predispositions operating more, as it were, from within (Œdipal jealousy, sibling rivalry or even genetic predisposition). The problem which therefore confronts the social scientist is that of trying to formulate in a particular area of behaviour some general propositions about the conditions under which a proportional influence should be assigned to each type of variable. Prediction, as cannot be too much emphasized, is never enough. Of course, we can predict elections, or formulate economic policies, or estimate population trends because we can treat such questions in the aggregate. In making assertions about the relevant systems (or sets of variables), we can assume that individual differences are being randomized out, just as an engineer can build a bridge by calculations of size or stress without taking account of the individual molecular occurrences of which his bridge is actually made. But the social scientist, even when he has discovered the most consistent correlations between aggregate data, has not given a full explanation until the personal factors of character and temperament have been assigned their relative weight. If we know, for example, even that 98 per cent of rich, Anglican, landowning stockbrokers vote Conservative, this only raises more acutely the problem of explaining the behaviour of the other 2 per cent. Attempts have been made with moderate success to correlate political behaviour with psychological as opposed to social factors. But we are a very long way from even an approximate estimate of the relative importance of the one as opposed to the other. It must be possible, at least, that a real advance may be made in this direction; or, to state it more cautiously still, if such an advance is about to be made it is likely to prove an exceedingly important one.

But this is speculative. The topics with which sociologists of politics are for the moment largely preoccupied are topics where a high degree of precision has only in very limited areas been attained. The vast amounts of data which their research is making available should not blind us to the realization that it must not be looked at as the cast-iron product of an infallible science holding true at all times and places, but rather as the raw material of political history which needs to be interpreted in its context. This is not, however, to say that it is impossible to make interesting generalizations about political behaviour and to test these by methods modelled, at least, on those of natural science. It is only to say, if you like, that though all sciences are sciences some will always remain more scientific than others; nor is there really any reason why even the partisans of social science should find this distressing.

CHAPTER II

THE EMERGENCE OF POLITICAL SOCIOLOGY

It is perhaps odd that modern political science should be as new an academic subject as it is; politics, after all, have been studied since before Aristotle, and political behaviour, if not as old as the objects of natural science, is nevertheless older than natural science itself. This newness, however, may be traced to the fact that the sociology of politics presupposes a distinction between the political and the social which is still recent in the history of ideas. Until this distinction, the sort of categorization which (as argued in chapter 1) is the necessary prerequisite to explanation could not be arrived at: before then, none of the writers about politics and the State saw quite why their subject need not in fact be coterminous with society itself. To see the emergence of the distinction we shall have to look briefly at some aspects of the history of European political thought. But it is also worth remembering how much of what we now mean when we talk about 'politics' is, in terms of European history, very recent indeed.

The principal change, of course, has been the enormous extension of the political over the last 150 years. Universal suffrage, large-scale bureaucracy, mass parties, are all recent institutions. Universal suffrage, it is as well to remember, dates in England only from 1929, in France from 1945 and in Belgium from 1949. Marx was dead before even the Third Reform Bill of 1885. Bentham, the foremost of the early champions of universal suffrage, died the day

The Emergence of Political Sociology

before the Reform Bill of 1832 received the royal assent. Bagehot's classic study *The English Constitution* was written under the imminence of the extended franchise of 1867, not based on an observation of its workings. France did have manhood suffrage for the whole second half of the nineteenth century, but nobody systematically studied how it operated; Proudhon, who remained the strongest doctrinal influence on French radical politics until after the Commune, merely dismissed it in a typical mixture of silliness and insight as 'a device to make the people lie'. Only in the United States can political democracy be regarded as an institution of reputably long standing: Tocqueville's famous study, *Democracy in America*, which he conceived after the fall of Charles X in 1830 and completed a decade later, remains the lonely forerunner of all our twentieth-century preoccupations with 'mass society'.

It is the same with the study of political parties. The two classics—Ostrogorski's *Democracy and the Organization of Political Parties* and Michels's *Political Parties*—appeared only at or after the turn of the century. The first study of the single party as a political institution did not appear until 1936. Even the topic of bureaucracy, though it is, like popular despotism, a worry to be found in Mill *On Liberty*, became a subject of generalized theoretical inquiry only with Max Weber.

Thus it is not surprising that an aura of novelty and even of naïveté still surrounds many of the topics with which contemporary sociologists of politics deal. It is perhaps even less surprising when we look also at the newness of many of their methods. One can, it is true, trace modern sociological methods right back to the 'Political Arithmetic' of the seventeenth century, when Sir William Petty, a Professor of Anatomy at Oxford who extended his interest also to the body politic, wrote his remarkable work on *The Political Anatomy of Ireland*. But modern statistical methods developed only in the late nineteenth century, and many are still more recent than this. The first International Statistical Congress did not meet until 1853; its chairman was the Belgian astronomer Quételet, who was not a sociologist by origin, but only later in his career took from Laplace the idea of applying probability theory to statistics about human populations. Sampling theory came into its own only shortly before the turn of the century, and techniques of statistical correlation only thereafter. In the *Journal of the Royal Statistical Society* during this period, there is a surprising amount of what nowadays would be called quantitative politics or sociology. But apart from what was relevant to the strictly biological sciences, nobody seems to have thought that this might constitute a separate academic subject; the various social surveys conducted in Britain were thought of as guides to public policy rather than topics which might one day be part of an autonomous university degree. Some techniques are more recent even than these. The notion that political or other attitudes might be in some sense measurable dates from the late 1920's in the United States; and sample survey data on voting is barely a quarter of a century old. For these reasons alone, it is not surprising that the 'scientific' study of politics should still be more productive of new questions than of answers to old ones.

But if we are really to understand the institutions and ideas which brought modern political sociology into being, we should properly go much farther back than this. We should, in fact, go right back to the period between Gerson and Grotius which J. N. Figgis, in a classic series of lectures delivered at Cambridge in 1900, first fully recog-

The Emergence of Political Sociology

nized as crucial. Between the failure of the Conciliar Movement at the beginning of the fifteenth century and the success of the Netherlands revolt some two hundred years later, the notion of territorial sovereignty had superseded the traditional belief in the theocratic unity of Christendom, and there had thereby begun to emerge the essential distinction, unthinkable in the Middle Ages, between society and the State. This could, at first sight, be regarded as no more than a reversion to Aristotle. Aristotle's *Politics* exercised an increasing influence from the mid thirteenth century onwards, and many of his generalizations (such as that a large middle class is the best guarantee against revolution) are precisely the sort of assertions that a modern political sociologist would dignify by the title of hypotheses. There is, however, an all-important difference. There is, in Aristotle, no distinction between social and political relations. 'Social', in English translations, is a rendering of πολιτικός; and the crucial contrast in Aristotle's mind is not between society and the State but between the private or familial and the political-cum-social. To ask either what is or should be the relation between society and the State is a question which could become meaningful only after the emergence of the modern idea of the State as such. This, as Figgis saw, must be principally credited to what can be called the unconscious alliance between Machiavelli and Luther.

Once, after this, the distinction begins to be realized, it should be possible to ask the question: which determines which? Is it, as sometimes implied by Machiavelli, the State (or rather, the statecraft of the prince) by which society is moulded, or is it, as explicitly stated in Marx, society which determines the form and nature of the State? The proper answer, of course, is that there is a reciprocal relation between the two; and it was perhaps Montesquieu who was the first important author to show an awareness of this, though there are hints of it even in Bodin. Montesquieu, for all the muddles rightly detected by his critics, saw both that social determinants affect the nature of government and also that society can be changed by precisely those rulers who understand the social determinants. But it was in general the problem of sovereignty which exercised the early theorists of the State, and their concern was rather to justify a prescriptive position than precisely to disentangle the causes and effects at work within the fabric of civil society. Hobbes, for example, in spite of all his hard-headed nominalism, is not a political sociologist as we would now understand the term. His social contract is not a sociological hypothesis but a historical model (even if he believed it) enlisted to bolster up a psychological model and the ethical theory implied by it. Indeed, we are here up against a second and different distinction, that between sociological and philosophical propositions. This is not, as already hinted, so absolute a distinction as has often been supposed. But until it became possible to see some explicit difference between thinking about politics in philosophical and sociological terms, any discussion of authority, or legitimacy, or the structure of rights and duties in the State could not but remain ambiguous. In fact, a real awareness of the distinction between political and social relations was not reached until very much later than the idea of the territorial State. This further awareness was, perhaps surprisingly, only reached in the 1840's.

It was, of course, latent a good deal earlier; but I want to suggest that it was no more than latent. In a sense, it underlay the whole transition from the exposition of natural law to the claim for natural rights which took place between Grotius and Rousseau. But Rousseau's famous contrast between man and citizen, fundamental though it is, is a contrast between man in a state of nature and man in civil society rather than between political man and social man. Similarly, Adam Ferguson, whose *History of Civil Society* was published four years after Rousseau's *Social Contract*, is sometimes excitedly claimed as the true precursor of modern sociology; but although (in a later work) he does define society as a generic term including both family and nation, this is only, like Aristotle or Aquinas or Althusius, to see the State as the all-embracing association and the family as a lesser one.[1] Ferguson does not, any more than Rousseau, properly distinguish social from political relations as such. I do not mean that Rousseau is not rightly credited with emphasizing the common humanity of men over and above their membership of a delimited citizen body. But this is not the same as seeing what we now understand as the distinction between society and the State.

A much stronger candidate is Saint-Simon—clumsy, naïve, far-sighted Saint-Simon, with his 'social physiology' and his 'Council of Newton' and his trust in the experts which nothing in his own life seems to justify. Saint-Simon is nowadays rightly conceded with intellectual priority over the actual inventor of the term 'sociology', his one-time associate Auguste Comte. For all his oddity, Saint-Simon's prescience is astonishing. All the intellectual preoccupations of the nineteenth century are foreshadowed in his writing: positivism, historicism, internationalism, industrialism, technocracy. Moreover, he was the first to see (for which Marx and Engels did give him some credit) that the economic structure of society is in some sense the basis for the form of the State: although (unlike Marx) he saw all institutions as the product of ideas, he did also see that 'l'économie politique est la véritable et unique fondement de la politique'. But the contrast throughout Saint-Simon's writing (though he is often not very clear) is between the 'political' and the 'social' only in the slightly special sense of the contrast between government and administration—the contrast which was later to recur still more drastically in Engels and Lenin. What Saint-Simon does is to try to take the politics out of government rather than describe how the governmental and political is related to the administrative and social. The society predicted by Saint-Simon is a sort of hierarchy of amiable expertise; he pictures subordination without coercion rather than the co-existence of the political and the social. The crux of the topic is there; but we are stopped short of a real empirical inquiry into the inter-relation of society and the State.

Similarly, it is because of their basic presupposition that the anarchists' contrast between society and government is not quite what I mean by the contrast between the social and the political. The radicalism of Paine or the anarchism of Godwin rest on an assumption by which the distinction is bound to be begged. Society, says Paine, is produced by our wants and government by our wickedness. Political government, says Godwin, is 'that brute engine which has been the only perennial cause of the vices of mankind'. This is the same distinction as Saint-Simon's, plus only the fiction of primordial innocence, and it can likewise be traced through Fourier and Owen to Marx, Engels and Lenin. But to say that government is the badge of lost innocence is to rule out by definition any discussion of coercion both legitimate and necessary; and it is this, as we shall see, that we must rely on if we are to distinguish the political as such.

The Emergence of Political Sociology

None of the anarchist writers (among whom even Proudhon should be included, although he preferred to call himself a 'socialist') realized that some form of political association is necessary to make societies possible at all, and that political relations must therefore co-exist with social relations although they need not necessarily overlap with them. Proudhon, for instance, thought that he could do away with what he meant by 'the State' and yet have constitutional guarantees for the rights that he wished to see recognized by society. All the anarchists, both before and after Saint-Simon, made a mistake very similar to this. They quite properly distinguished co-operation from coercion, and administration from government; but they went on from this (as Marx did, but from different premisses) to advocate a sort of non-political government without seeing that this is either a contradiction in terms or else an unargued over-optimism about human nature.

Society cannot, as Godwin wished it to do, restrict its coercive sanctions to the intermittent restraint of incurable criminals. Social organization presupposes that some people must have some power over some other people which is recognized by enough of all the people as legitimate; and thus competition for power must somehow be regulated or institutionalized. An understanding of how social institutions co-exist with political is much more evident in Tocqueville's discussion of the importance of voluntary associations in American democracy. But Tocqueville never follows out the implications of his discussion. To see what looks (up to the 1840's) most like an explicit discussion of the State as distinct from society we must glance at least briefly at the most famous of Saint-Simon's contemporaries, who died only six years after Saint-Simon but appears never to have been read by him: I refer, of course, to Hegel.

In the *Philosophy of Right*, which he published in 1821, Hegel takes explicit pains to warn us against confusing the state with 'civil society'. He also emphasizes that 'particular interests which are common to everyone fall within civil society and lie outside the absolutely universal interest of the state proper'.[1] But again this is not quite what is needed. Hegel's error is that although he appears to be saying that civil society is something separate, he at the same time makes the State's interest 'absolutely universal' by definition. He means not that civil society is something separate from the State, but rather that without the State civil society is incomplete. For Hegel, civil society is simply a lesser form of State. He subsumes society under the State as a sort of inferior predicate, very much as Comte subsumes the State under society. Hegel means in fact too much by 'the State': he seems sometimes (though by no means always) to understand by it more what Malinowski means by 'culture' or Durkheim means by the 'collective consciousness'. It still, of course, retains its inherently political meaning; but this is just the trouble. Hegel never saw that the social and the political can co-exist in juxtaposition or even in opposition, and that the problem to be considered is the relation between the political and the separate, non-political element in 'civil society'. The question which needs to be asked depends on an explicit separation of society and the State in terms not formulated until Marx's criticism of Hegel and the important but less notorious writings of Marx's contemporary Lorenz von Stein.

It is difficult for the mid-twentieth-century reader to appreciate the upheaval involved in the post-Hegelian intellectual revolution. Historians of ideas have often stressed it: but it is still an effort to understand, let alone to re-create, the enormous and suffocating influence which

Hegel exercised even on those authors who most self-consciously rebelled against him. This is no less true, as Sartre and others have reminded us, of Kierkegaard than of Marx. Indeed, it was what made Hegel's system so impressive an intellectual achievement that also made it so much of a struggle to break out of: its all-embracingness. This meant not only that its influence was nowhere really escapable; it also meant that once somebody had successfully challenged a part of it then its total validity must collapse, even though its influence might still outlast its validity. Hegel's successors were all writing in their different fashions under his influence, but at the same time none of them could feel that it was any longer under his regime.

The first demolition took some time—in fact, a decade after Hegel was dead; but when it happened, it happened with a bang. Elsewhere in Europe the early 1840's were also yielding a startling crop of important works: in France, Comte brought out the final volume of his *Cours de Philosophie Positive*, and Proudhon issued his famous pronouncement that 'Property is Theft'; in England, J. S. Mill brought out his *System of Logic*, whose sixth book contains what is still a standard discussion of method in social science. But it was in Germany that the ferment was most intense. Not only Marx but also Feuerbach, Kierkegaard, Stirner and von Stein produced works between 1841 and 1844 which when taken together signify the self-conscious, definitive and explicit replacement of the Hegelian system.

It can be argued that the reaction against the specifically religious element in Hegel's system is both bound up with and more important than the reaction against his political theory. Certainly, this is why Feuerbach and Kierkegaard are in their opposite ways so important; and there is much of

Marx that one cannot understand without taking account of his atheism. Since, however, I am concerned chiefly with the distinction of politics as a separate and autonomous subject, I shall leave the religious element aside. A full analysis of the distinction between society and the State can first be seen in Marx's early criticisms of Hegel. Marx had completed his doctoral thesis in 1841. Initially a student of law, then a convert to philosophy, he had been the ablest of the members of the Berlin University *Doktorklub* who had become first immersed in and then dissatisfied with Hegelian theology. Deprived of an academic career by an official clamp-down on the 'Left Hegelians' and of independent means by his father's sudden death, Marx went to Cologne and contributed to the *Rheinische Zeitung* the series of articles which constitute his first political writings. In this same period he wrote two critiques of Hegel. One, the *Kritik der Hegelschen Staatsrecht*, did not appear in print at all until long after Marx was dead; but it gives a valuable insight into his early awareness of just that failing in Hegel's political theory of which I have been speaking. The work is still not available in English. But a single paragraph is worth quoting in full, after which I shall try to say what I think Marx means by it.

'Hegel's profundity', says Marx, 'lies in his view of the separation of civil and political society as a contradiction. But he is wrong in that he contents himself with the semblance of its resolution and passes the semblance off for the real thing. The fact is that the "so-called theories" which he despises demand the separation of civil and political status; and rightly so, since they articulate one of the consequences of modern society, namely that now the element of political stratification is nothing other than the factual

The Emergence of Political Sociology

The Emergence of Political Sociology

expression of the actual relation between the State and civil society, that is, their separation.'[1]

The 'so-called theories' which are referred to as arousing Hegel's contempt are theories of a distinction between social and political classes; and what I take Marx to be saying is that the political hierarchy is in fact separate from though interrelated with the non-political organization of society, so that for Hegel to assert their fusion as a necessary (and indeed desirable) fact is to force a metaphysical harmony upon an empirically real contradiction. This shift of emphasis is crucial. It does not mean that Marx himself altogether sheds either metaphysics or Utopian anarchism; but whether or not Marx is quite as scientific as he sometimes pretends, we can still see throughout his work the effective and explicit empirical distinction between society and the State. Marx agrees with the anarchists that the State is a wicked imposition; but, unlike them, he offers a full-scale analysis of how and why it is related to society under different economic conditions. One need not believe that the relation between society and the State is exactly what Marx thinks it is. But he is aware both of the difference between them and of the separate difference between a sociological and a metaphysical discussion of politics. On the relation between Marx's own philosophy and sociology of politics, I shall say more in the following chapter. For the moment, I want only to emphasize that it is not until Marx and von Stein that a real sociology of politics becomes conceivable.

Von Stein is, of course, a great deal less famous than Marx, and the extent of his influence on Marx is not certain. It may be from him that Marx acquired his notion of the proletariat, but as far as I know this has not been definitely established one way or the other by Marxian scholars. In any event, the question of priorities is not all that important. What is interesting is that it has been claimed on von Stein's behalf (and indeed he at one point claims himself) that he was the first author to discuss society as an independent concept.[1] There is not much sign of this in his first book, a study of socialism and communism in France, which appeared in 1842. But the expanded version which von Stein published under a different title in 1850 contains in its introductory section a discussion of some length on the relation between society and the State. 'The principle of the State', says von Stein, 'stands in direct opposition to the principle of society'; and again, 'The character of the life of a people is the continuous struggle between the State and society'.[2] This is almost exactly the sort of argument we find in Marx's writings of the same period. 'The State is founded', he writes in 1844, 'upon the contradiction between public and private life'; and in 1845, 'only political superstition believes nowadays that civil life must be held together by the State when in fact the State is upheld by civil life'.[3] Von Stein is perhaps not so far from Hegel as Marx is, and I am certainly not suggesting that he is comparable to Marx in originality. But he is worth citing together with Marx as signifying the emergence of a distinction which had been only latent or metaphysical before, and which now and only now makes possible a sociology of politics.

I have implied, however, that Marx's notion of the State, though it distinguishes it from society, will still not quite do. And since we need to define the State (and thereby, or in addition, the political) if we are to be clear what our subject-matter is supposed to be, I had now better offer the definition I propose to use. To do this, I shall start, as in chapter 1, from Max Weber. This is not because Weber's

The Emergence of Political Sociology

definitions will quite do either, but because a modification of Weber's definition in the light of three later criticisms will yield the most useful result. I shall therefore begin by quoting Weber (not, in fact, exactly as written, but by running together his most important assertions on these topics).

'But what', asks Weber, 'is a "political" association from the sociological point of view? What is a State? Sociologically, the State cannot be defined in terms of what it does. There is scarcely any task that some political association has not taken in hand, and there is no task that one could say has always been exclusive and peculiar to those associations which are designated as political. Ultimately, one can give a sociological definition of the modern state only in terms of the specific means peculiar to it, as to every political association, namely, the use of physical force. If the only social institutions which existed did not know the use of violence, then the concept of "State" would disappear, and there would emerge what could be designated "anarchy" in the specific sense of the word. A State is a human community which successfully claims within a given territory the monopoly of the legitimate use of physical force. Hence, "politics" means to us striving to share power or to influence the distribution of power, either among States or among groups within a State. When a question is said to be a "political" question, what is always meant is that the decisive criterion for its answer is interests in the distribution, maintenance or transfer of power.'

All this is excellent. It shows Weber at his most lucid and cogent, and it is backed up, like all Weber's discussions, with an encyclopaedic scholarship unrivalled in social science. But it is still not quite what we need. The first objection to be overcome is due to the political anthropologists, who have since Weber's day given us accounts of societies which are not anarchic but where there is no centralized monopoly of the legitimate use of force. Professor Schapera, in his lectures on *Government and Politics in Tribal Societies* (1956), stresses that the public life of the Bergdama or the Bushmen, though not fulfilling Weber's definition of a 'State', is still 'subject to a definite system of control, and is neither chaotic nor casual in operation'. Are we not, therefore, in trying to follow Weber, likely to impose where it is not suitable a terminology derived from and only appropriate to the territorial political units of Western Europe? In fact I do not think so, for all we have to be prepared to do is to talk about 'stateless' societies (as Weber does in the case of medieval Europe)—societies, that is, where force may be used but where there is no recognized central monopoly of it. This enables us to retain the undoubted value of Weber's definition without going against the ordinary use of 'State', which does imply the notion of centralization. Apart, however, from the centralized monopoly objection, there are two other qualifications which need to be made to Weber's definition, one trivial, but the other more important. Both, curiously enough, can be found in the work of the greatest of Weber's sociological contemporaries, Émile Durkheim; and I say 'curiously' not only because Durkheim is not normally thought of as a writer on politics but because he and Weber, just like Hegel and Saint-Simon before them, appear to have worked contemporaneously but independently of each other.

Durkheim is known chiefly for his work on topics more social than political—suicide, religion, the division of labour, and the methods and philosophy of social science. He did write three studies of political thinkers—Montesquieu, Rousseau and Saint-Simon—where his elegance

The Emergence of Political Sociology

of mind and cogency are shown in some ways to best advantage; but on the whole he was much less concerned with politics than Weber was. He did, however, in his long unpublished lectures on *Professional Ethics and Civic Morals*, discuss at some length the definition of the State. The first point I want to borrow from him is, as I have warned, a trivial one. None the less, it reads almost as though it were specifically directed against Weber's definition: 'Where', says Durkheim, 'cardinal importance attaches to national territory, it is of comparatively recent date. To begin with, it seems rather arbitrary to deny any political character to the great nomad societies whose structure was sometimes very elaborate.'[1] This is surely fair. We can, of course, retain Weber's emphasis on territorial unity by denying the title of 'State' even to centralized and organized nomadic tribes. It seems better, however, to keep centralization alone as the criterion, and to drop territory, so that we can, if we have to, talk not only about 'stateless societies' but about 'non-territorial States'. The remaining qualification, however, is rather more important, for the principal deficiency in Weber's analysis is just the contrast with which I began this chapter—Aristotle's basic contrast between the public and the private which has among recent authors been most emphatically revived by Miss Hannah Arendt.

There is no great point in particularly following Durkheim here, since I cited him less because I want to agree with him than because it is interesting that it should be he who says what he does. Durkheim's failing, as his critics have rightly detected, is that he surreptitiously reimposes a capital S on society instead of talking about societies as such. He thus comes most of the way back to Comte, whom he has so carefully denounced, and like Comte tends to smother the State in Society itself. Durkheim does, however, make two essential points. First of all, he stresses that a patriarchal family, though it may be a social unit containing both governors and governed, is not a State; secondly, he emphasizes that the idea of the State presupposes the existence of other social groupings under it. Durkheim's actual definition of the State is not what we want, since it involves his own suspect notion of 'collective representations'. However, the essentially public aspect of the State (and the political) is brought out by him, and it is this that I want to stress. To talk about political relations, even in stateless societies, is to talk about relations on the public side of the private/public line. If political organization is synonymous with familial organization, then it is not political. The family is not a political unit, whether it rests on legitimate force or not, and a society where every family was politically autonomous would not be a society, but only a clan-ridden territory in a state of anarchy. Weber does, it is true, get at much the same point in his emphasis on the role of an administrative staff in the exercise of political power. But we want to add to Weber's definition of the political an explicit emphasis on the public/private distinction. With this, we have what is perhaps the best definition of what 'political sociology' is about.[1]

There is still the slight difficulty with the political/social contrast that since the social is, as I stressed in my first chapter, a category embracing the political, economic, religious and all other collective areas of behaviour, to distinguish the social and political may seem either a tautology or a paradox. But what is meant by social is, of course, in this context, all that is social and not political. This must include (as well as the economic, etc.) the sort of residual category of social relations that cannot be covered by any other more specific term: such forms of relation as friend-

The Emergence of Political Sociology

ship are the sort most naturally describable only as 'social' relations. But once this is clear, it is not worth going into any more terminological contortions. There is only one more point to be stressed *à propos* of defining the political, and that is Weber's warning against trying to define the State by what it does.

This is important because many people, notably the so-called 'functionalists' whom I shall return to in chapter VI, have tried and still do try to do just this. Weber himself, to make it worse, is in fact mistranslated in the standard English version, for 'what it does' is for some reason turned into 'its ends'. To define the State by what it does is dangerous not only because of Weber's point that there is scarcely anything the State does not do. It is also dangerous on simple logical grounds. If the State is defined by what it does, then first, it must cease to be a State if it doesn't, and second, anything which does what States do must be a State. Up to a point this is all right, for even in Weber's definition—which rests rather on means—if a State ceases to retain its recognized monopoly of force then we wish to say it is no longer a State. But beyond this, there are obvious snags. When, for instance, Hobhouse (writing in 1924) defines the State as 'the community organized for certain [governmental] purposes'[1] he lands himself back in the Hegelian blur between society and the State which (as Durkheim did with Comte) he started out by criticizing. Of course, it is Hobhouse's 'community' which makes his definition particularly flaccid, for (just as with Hegel) it enables him quietly to by-pass the problem of legitimacy which Weber rightly emphasizes. But even if he had defined the State only as that part of the community which does certain things for certain purposes, the weakness of such a definition remains: sooner or later (unless the definition is tautological) one will find a State that doesn't do them or some other institution that does but that cannot be convincingly described as political. Hobhouse is one of those authors who would have been a much better sociologist if he had been a better philosopher, and vice versa: and perhaps the moral to be drawn is that one should always be a little suspicious when a sociological definition of the State is offered in support of what is going to be a philosophical argument.

The same mistake, however, is made by some of the most scientistically minded practitioners of American political science. I quote, for instance, from Professor Gabriel Almond, writing in 1960: 'What we [Professors Almond and Coleman] propose is that the political system is that system of interactions to be found in all independent societies which performs the functions of integration and adaptation (both internally and *vis à vis* other societies) by means of the employment, or threat of employment, of more or less legitimate physical compulsion.'[1] Professors Almond and Coleman are arguing as self-confessed functionalists, and although functionalism has always been in logically dubious health I am not trying to deny that (as Almond and Coleman themselves demonstrate) it cannot be an interesting and useful approach. But what does it mean specifically to define the political system by its functions (i.e., by what it does)? Once again, the same unanswered question poses itself: suppose the State chooses to use its legitimate coercive means for functions that are not integrative or adaptive (however those two equally dangerous terms are defined)? Does it then cease to be the State? We must presumably say that it does; but this means that our definition has turned into another of the many tautologies that have proved a perennial weakness of functionalism. If the

The Emergence of Political Sociology

State does whatever it does by definition, then the proposition that 'the (or a) State does X' is no longer an empirical one. What in fact we want to do (and by Weber's definition are enabled to) is to consider empirically what is or is not done by those institutions which have legitimate coercion at their disposal; this is no use at all if what we mean by the State depends on the 'integrative' or 'adaptive' results of what it does.

Thus we shall do better to remain with Weber's form of definition as well as with a qualified version of its content. Since I shall be saying more about functionalism later on, I shall not take the tautology point any further. But it is essential to emphasize that the criterion of the 'political' is means and not results. The subject-matter of political sociology is therefore all those institutions and behaviour which on the basis of the foregoing discussion can be labelled 'political'. This will include the reciprocal relations between the political and the social (in the sense of all other 'social' institutions and behaviour not subsumed also under the political). The political is thus not entailed by the social, but it does entail, in a sense which I hope is now clear, both the coercive and the public. This sort of discussion, I have suggested, did not really become explicit or feasible until after Hegel; and it is thus only for a little over a century that political sociology has been a definite and distinguishable subject.

There is one final point to be made about this definition. I have been emphasizing the emergence of politics not only as an autonomous but also as an empirical study, and though the two more or less coincide in Marx's rejection of Hegel the issues involved are very different. As argued in chapter 1, the most remorseless empiricism still cannot make politics a science in the strict positivistic sense, and while the autonomy of political studies has been a useful development it has, perhaps, been partly responsible for the positivistic excesses of some of its practitioners. The logical relation between a (more or less empirical) proposition in political sociology and a (more or less prescriptive) proposition in political philosophy is a complicated and intractable problem which I shall have to return to in the final chapter. But in tracing the emergence of political sociology I do not want to have implied that even if purged of positivism it necessarily controverts, let alone replaces, the sorts of utterance made by the traditional political theorists. Often, of course, it does controvert the traditional theorists, who not only lacked the evidence they needed but were trying more to justify the state of affairs they wanted to see realized than to ask what social conditions might produce or result from it. But this does not mean that what we find in the pages of Hobbes, or Bentham, or Mill has been superseded, like alchemy by chemistry, by the results of political science. Political theory remains a separate, philosophical discipline which neither the positivism of political science nor that of linguistic analysis has outmoded, though they both may have been very good for it. On the other hand, that there has always been a necessary link between empirical conclusions about politics and political theories (or philosophies) is the central theme of these essays.

CHAPTER III

KARL MARX AND MAX WEBER

Of all the authors who have contributed to the sociology of politics since it was effectively founded by Marx, only Weber can stand serious comparison with Marx himself. I do not mean, however, by discussing them together to set them as it were into public competition. It is true that Weber wrote much of his work as a conscious qualification or rejoinder to Marx, and remains best known for his discussion of the role of ideas in history which he put forward as a direct counter-claim against dialectical materialism. But much of his contribution to the sociology of politics can be looked at apart from its relation to Marxism. The interest of both Marx and Weber to my argument does not depend on an adjudication of their respective merits, but rather on the nature of their respective claims to scientific objectivity for their conclusions. What I shall try to do, in the light of this common issue, is to consider the relation between their sociology and their philosophy of politics.

The basic outlines of Marx's work are too well known to need recapitulation. But what is worth remarking for our present purpose is that Marx at no point makes quite such sweeping claims to scientific validity as are several times made by Engels (and subsequently Lenin) on his behalf. This is particularly true of his earlier writings. Many of these remained unpublished during his lifetime, and indeed were regarded by Engels as much less important than the amplification and elaboration of the Theory of Surplus Value on which Marx was working when he died. But

Marx's early work has received increasing attention since the 1920's, due to a large extent to a volume of essays published in 1923 (in German) by the Hungarian Marxist Georg Lukacs under the title *History and Class-Consciousness*. Lukacs, who was a pupil of Weber's as well as a student of Marx, is sometimes described as the most original Marxist since Marx himself. He was at once attacked, after publishing *History and Class-Consciousness*, for emasculating the materialism out of dialectical materialism, and he was subsequently forced (or, perhaps, not entirely forced) to recant when he fled from Hitler's Germany to Stalin's Russia in the 1930's.[1] But the publication of more of Marx's early writings than were available in the 1920's has largely vindicated the interpretation which Lukacs inferred from Marx's later work. Lukacs himself, though commanding a steadily increasing reputation both as a literary critic and a philosopher, has continued to disown the views he expressed in 1923. But he remains one of the chief contributors to the reappraisal of Marx as a philosophical humanist which was subsequently taken up by the revisionists of the 1950's.

It is hard to dispute that both Marx and Engels, in their later exposition of their views, were enunciating a doctrine which reads very differently from the moralistic, satirical and essentially philosophical tone of what Marx was writing in the early and middle 1840's. To contrast the earliest with the latest writings of Marx (and their interpretation by Engels) is to be struck at once by a paradox. On the one hand, Marx becomes much more scientific: the polemic is still there, but it is imbedded in a mounting heap of economic data and analysis. The Theory of Surplus Value is expounded and reiterated, but purely philosophical discussion disappears almost altogether, and both Marx and

Engels draw the explicit analogy between the work of Marx and the work of Darwin. At the same time, however, both Marx and Engels are concerned to modify the over-mechanistic interpretation which can be placed on Marx's work. Engels was able in the 1890's to talk about younger Marxists placing more emphasis on the economic factor than is due to it, and Marx himself is credited in later life with the famous remark that 'Je ne suis pas Marxiste'. How, therefore, should we reconcile the two?

Perhaps the readiest answer is simply to emphasize that Marx, even at his most philosophical, was still (or already) a materialist. In his writings prior to 1847 he was arguing most of the time (though not, to be strictly accurate, quite always) as a conscious and self-styled materialist.[1] Although the phrase 'historical materialism' is not his own—it was first used by Engels—Marx explicitly saw himself as the clear-eyed, hard-headed opponent of a vaporous Hegelian idealism. In his fierce attacks on the 'young Hegelians', which even Engels thought at some points excessive, he is savagely contemptuous of what he refers to as 'old Hegelian junk'. Moreover, he is as scornful of Utopian socialists as he is of Hegelian idealists. '*The sole point*', he writes in a well-known letter of 1846,[2] 'on which I am in complete agreement with Monsieur Proudhon is in his dislike for sentimental socialist daydreams.' Logically enough, Marx and Engels continued to welcome any signs of impending economic crisis, for bankruptcies and crop failures are the surest harbingers of impending revolution. Humanitarianism, Marx seems often to be saying, is at best irrelevant; at worst, it is positively harmful.

But we are still confronted by a paradox. As his commentators have been quick to observe, Marx is both more of a metaphysician and also more of a Utopian than he is apt to pretend. He attacks Proudhon for being 'doctrinaire';[1] but is Proudhon really any more doctrinaire than Marx himself? He savages the cloudy abstractions of Hegelian metaphysics; but he also attacks what he calls 'vulgar' materialism. He talks in his preface to the second edition of *Capital* about turning the dialectic right side up again;[2] but after all, as Marx explicitly avows, it is still the dialectic. Moreover, it is impossible to read very much of Marx without becoming aware of reading something a good deal more emotive than a scientific treatise. The sheer force of moral indignation which reverberates throughout *Capital* is not the least reason for its influence; and equally, such hints as Marx gives of the future society which will emerge from the expropriation of the expropriators are as Utopian in their way as the visions of Fourier or Cabet. Marx hesitates neither to condemn the capitalists nor, for example, to praise the impartiality of the factory inspectors or the 'simple moral sense' of Rousseau. Marx, in fact, is never any less of a moralist because he is also, or primarily, a scientific materialist.

These contradictions are familiar to every reader of Marx, and are exhaustively dealt with by his commentators. But what is important for my present purpose is precisely to stress to what extent in Marx's writings statements of prescription and statements of fact are inextricably linked. It is this which provides the key to reconciling the paradox of the 'philosophical' and the 'scientific' Marx. If it is true that Marx was an anti-Hegelian materialist during his most philosophical period, it is also true that at his most scientific he was still a philosopher whose greatest intellectual debt was to Hegel. To Marx himself, indeed, statements of prescription and of fact are by definition inseparable. Marx is the founder of what has since come to be known as the

Karl Marx and Max Weber

sociology of knowledge, and he seems sometimes to consider not only economic or political thought but even the most factual or technical knowledge to be governed by the economic substructure. Marx and Engels are not always consistent on this subtle and amorphous topic, which I shall touch on again in chapter VIII. But it can be cogently argued that Marx is himself a paradigm for his own contention of the inextricable link between fact and value. Even though we may agree with him in conceding to natural, if not to economic, science a higher objective validity than to what he calls the 'legal, political, religious, aesthetic or philosophical—in short ideological forms', we can still use an argument very similar to his own to show that his political and economic doctrine is not and can never be a natural science. Of all Marx's innumerable commentators, the point is perhaps most strikingly made by Durkheim. 'Socialism', says Durkheim, 'is not a science, a sociology in miniature—it is a cry of pain, sometimes of anger, uttered by men who feel most keenly our collective *malaise*.'[1]

The best and, in the view of many commentators, the focal illustration of this is Marx's famous concept of alienation, which has received so much attention in recent years as almost to smother the rest of the enormous secondary literature on Marxism. I am not here concerned either to try to say what Marx 'really' meant by alienation, or to trace his adaptation of the term through Hegel via Feuerbach. What I want to emphasize is that on any plausible interpretation the term has both a philosophical and a sociological content. Philosophically, what Marx means by alienation is (however we are to understand this) a process of 'objectification' which estranges men from themselves, each other and the world. Sociologically, however, it has a twofold content (at least—but this will be enough for my argument):[1] first, alienation is the loss by man of identification with his work and his products—that is, they become an embodiment of his labour set over against himself; second, alienation is the setting of men against each other in a form of social relations unnaturally engendered by the compulsions of political economy. In both these two senses, the economic and the social, alienation is linked to the system of private property in a reciprocal causal relation, although initially it is alienation which causes private property, not, as one would perhaps expect, the other way round. This raises difficulties which I shall not go into: Marx in a different passage places the origin of the division of labour in the sexual act, so that the biological determinants of family life must perhaps be seen as entailing a kind of primal alienation. But apart from the difficulty of being certain what exactly Marx meant, two points are at once apparent. First, if there are sociological grounds for rejecting Marx's hypotheses of cause and effect, then the ethical argument embodied in the notion of alienation must be sharply modified. But second, if there are philosophical grounds for rejecting Marx's interpretation of work and labour, then the sociological hypotheses, if true, remain so only in a different and more limited sense than that intended by Marx.

To illustrate this, it will be enough to cite the standard objections to Marx's economic postulates. Although he asserts in the *Economic and Philosophical Manuscripts of 1844* that 'it is hardly necessary to assure the reader conversant with political economy that my results have been won by means of a wholly empirical analysis',[2] there are three separate but interconnected parts of his argument which his critics have subjected to strong empirical criticism: the effects of the division of labour, the possibility of abolishing private property and the historical role of the proletariat.

First of all, objection is made to Marx's account of the division of labour, or rather of its effects. Apart from the ambiguities of his account, we may ask whether it need in any case be always true that 'whilst the division of labour raises the productive power of labour and increases the wealth and refinement of society it impoverishes the worker and reduces him to a machine'.[1] May it not be the case that the division of labour has produced this result only because of actual policies of distribution and exchange which, if modified, would cause the division of labour to enrich the worker rather than to impoverish him? If the division and specialization of labour is necessary (which it surely is) to the general prosperity of the community, is it really feasible to posit—as Marx and Engels do in the *German Ideology*—a Communist society in which 'society regulates the general production and thus makes it possible for me to do one thing today and another tomorrow, to hunt in the morning, fish in the afternoon, rear cattle in the evening, criticize after dinner, just as I have a mind, without ever becoming hunter, fisherman, shepherd or critic'?[2] Secondly, is it in any case possible to abolish private property altogether? Marx is notoriously vague about the working details of the Communist society. But unless his general aim is really attainable, and unless, moreover, his proposed methods are the only ones whereby it can be put into effect, then his political philosophy must be proportionately modified. Certainly, it is our duty to work for the overthrow of the end-product of political alienation which is the bourgeois State provided, first, that this will in fact bring about the optimal state of affairs, and second, that this is the only way to bring it about. But both these provisions are disputable. Finally, as Marx's critics have triumphantly reiterated during the Western progression towards affluence, the proletariat has not, as predicted, been growing proportionately larger and poorer. Can we, if only for this reason, be sure of doing the best possible thing if we still direct all our political efforts towards revolution? All this is thoroughly well-trodden ground. But the moral, whatever one's point of view, is that if empirical objections can be sustained against what Marx puts forward as empirical argument, then one's assent to his prescriptive assertions may have to be sharply modified.

But suppose we now look from the philosophical end at the connection between Marx's sociology and philosophy of politics. If we look at all closely at the words which Marx uses in his discussion of the labour process, we see at once that the meaning and thereby the validity of what he describes as his empirical analysis depends upon the interpretation given to certain crucial terms. Alienation itself can, as we have seen, be given a concrete sociological meaning with reference to the worker's relations both (economically) to the products of his labour and (socially) to the persons controlling the conditions of the labour process. But it remains nonetheless a philosophical concept deriving from a philosophical notion of the proper nature of man. The word 'dehumanization' is crucial here. There is, of course, a sense in which we want to describe the condition of the industrial workers under mid-Victorian capitalism in this kind of terms, meaning simply that for human beings to have had to live and work like this is repugnant to our moral sense. But Marx means more than this. He talks in such phrases as the worker 'estranging himself from himself'; he rests his argument on his notion of the nature of man as a 'generic' or 'species being' (the difficult word *Gattungswesen*); and, most importantly of all, there underlies the whole position which he puts forward what can only be described as a philosophy of work itself.

Sometimes, Marx talks as though he wishes to abolish work (or labour) altogether; and these remarks have led Miss Arendt in *The Human Condition* to accuse Marx of leaving us with 'the rather distressing alternative between productive slavery and unproductive freedom'.[1] This, however, is not quite fair. Several passages can be cited to show that what Marx means is not so much the abolition of all work but the abolition of the division of labour in its present form. He says clearly in *Capital* of a community of free individuals that 'all the characteristics of Robinson Crusoe's labour are here repeated, but with this difference, that they are social instead of individual'.[2] The society we have already seen envisaged in the *German Ideology* does, as Miss Arendt aptly puts it, turn all professions into hobbies; but they are still productive hobbies. Nor is it the case, as Miss Arendt maintains, that Marx rests his definition of man on man as labourer instead of as reasoner, for he emphasizes that what distinguishes man from the animals is not merely labour but what he calls 'self-conscious life-activity'. What is, however, entirely true is that Marx's discussion does rest on a notion of the essential nature and proper activities of man. He speaks of alienation as reversing the relationship which distinguishes man from the animals precisely by making man's essential being a mere means to his animal existence; he regards private property as incompatible with what he explicitly calls 'human status and dignity'; and he regards the proper character of work to be—as we saw from the quotation from *Capital*—'social', by which he means not merely communal, for he says (perhaps surprisingly) that 'when I am active scientifically... then I am active socially, because I am active as *man*'.[3]

My concern is not to evaluate these arguments in detail. But the more closely one looks at them, the clearer it becomes how much of their force derives precisely from their not being couched in entirely neutral or scientific terms. A good analogy is the description of a topic which Marx also touches on, namely prostitution. This is a social phenomenon which can be described in purely clinical terms; but these carry the feeling that this is an incomplete description precisely because we wish to use words reflecting a difference between prostitution and 'normal' or 'natural' sexual relations. This applies exactly to Marx's view of work. To Marx, there is a 'natural' way for mankind to carry out the productive processes necessary for his survival and well-being, and it is this which provides the yardstick against which capitalism is seen to be dehumanizing and therefore wrong. We are confronted with just Max Weber's (and Professor Hampshire's) problem of choice of words. Marx's most vehement protestations of empirical method do not alter Weber's central point that the construction of the vocabulary to be used in any such investigation depends upon the underlying point of view. This is the central tenet of Weber's doctrine of method; and with it we may appropriately turn from Marx to Weber himself, and to the consideration of the relation between Weber's philosophy and sociology of politics.

To turn from Marx to Weber is to exchange a blitzkrieg for siege-warfare. None of Weber's writings has the brutal power of the *Communist Manifesto* or the purple passages of *Capital*. Weber's tone is almost always impartial, his erudition suffocating and his striking phrases few and far between. Nobody can ever have said of Weber what Bernard Shaw is supposed to have said after reading *Capital*: 'Karl Marx made a man of me.' Weber founded no

Karl Marx and Max Weber

school of doctrinaire disciples and he has had no 'ism' named after him. But perhaps it is only because his evidence is so diverse, his reasoning so complex and his conclusions so carefully qualified that his influence by comparison with that of Marx has been almost negligible. Reading Weber, one's first two impressions are of the breadth of his learning and the difficulty of his style. He is alleged to have asked on one occasion why it should be easier for his readers to read his works than it was for him to write them; and his private life—although, like Marx, he had a devoted wife, and, unlike Marx, no financial problems—is a spasmodic history of insomnia, neurosis and breakdown. When, however, one perseveres through his definitions and elaborations, his compulsive repetitions and qualifications, one comes to realize that he is not only Marx's superior in breadth of historical knowledge but also at least his equal in intellectual power.

Some aspects of Weber's voluminous researches are altogether outside the province of these essays, and some I shall be returning to in chapters VII and VIII. For the moment, I want only to look, as with Marx, at the relation between Weber's sociology and (if he has one) philosophy of politics. As we have seen from his views of sociological method, Weber is as ready as Marx to claim for his studies the status of science, and like Marx he sees that there is a fundamental connection between social values and social science. But his claim is very differently based. For Marx, social science and social values are mutually involved because all social thought is liable to be (in his sense of the term) 'ideological'; for Weber, they are involved because the social sciences must be 'value-relevant', although this does not prevent the conduct of an actual sociological investigation from being 'value-free'.

We must begin, says Weber, by seeing that our fundamental standpoint is arbitrary; but we must follow it up in accordance with the canons of objective science. What Weber did, as one of his shrewdest critics, Professor Aron, has pointed out, was first to admit the plurality of possible interpretations, but then to do all he could to reduce the consequences of this fact.[1] This raises some difficulties, as Aron makes clear and as we shall soon see. But initially Weber seems to start from a stronger position than Marx. Marx's claims to objective science cannot be wholly tenable, and indeed if they were, they might diminish their own effect, since it is the philosophical content of Marx's arguments that gives them much of their force. Weber, by contrast, seems to do better on this score. Having conceded at the outset the influence which value-judgements must have on any investigation in the social sciences, he can proceed to what, with this sole reservation, is an objective and impartial discussion of topics as diverse as the German stock exchange, Confucianism and the social foundations of music. But we must ask nevertheless the two standard questions: first, is Weber's political sociology value-free in quite the way that he lays down? and second, what might be its prescriptive implications for a non-Marxist philosophy of politics?

The best comparison, as far as I know, between Marx and Weber is an essay by Karl Löwith which appeared in 1932—twelve years after Weber's premature death from pneumonia—in the penultimate issue of the periodical which Weber himself had edited.[2] Löwith, although emphasizing that Marx offers a cure for society where Weber's analysis is carefully limited to a diagnosis, also makes the important point that there underlies Weber's analysis, just as there does Marx's, a view not only *about* but also *of* man; and he shows how the concept of 'rationalization' can be assigned as crucial a role in Weber's schema as 'alienation' in Marx's. Weber's use of the word 'disenchantment' (*Entzauberung*) is significant. His view of history is as a successive process of secularization, formalization and bureaucratization, and—as he is aware—his analysis, being a product of the end-stage of this process, is a sort of turning-back of the process on itself. Is it, therefore, possible for Weber to apply his 'disenchanted' analysis in a way that is not itself evaluatively biased and historically relative?

It is a frequent accusation against Weber that he fails to follow his own recommendations about method. To some of his critics this is a good thing rather than otherwise, but it is either way hard to dispute that Weber's historical writing is less wholly free of subjective interpretation than his remarks about method might suggest. For despite the apparent advantage of conceding at the outset that basic standpoints are arbitrary, Weber in fact confronts himself with a dilemma because of the simple difficulty that he quite obviously doesn't believe this: his own basic standpoint is a belief in as 'scientific' an objectivity as possible, and many of his remarks make it clear that he would like to make his historical vocabulary 'value-free' despite (or as well as) his concession of its 'value-relevance'. This has a double disadvantage in practice, for not only does objectivity not follow from the concession that standpoints are arbitrary, but the standard which Weber implies is quite impossible to live up to. Weber's doctrine of 'value-relevance' entitles him to his own 'value-free' standpoint; but it deprives him of any criterion for saying that it is a better standpoint than any other. However, it can perhaps be said on Weber's behalf that this is a sophistic criticism. Given that a value-free standpoint is itself relative and arbitrary, to be sceptical about it is still as academic an objection as to be sceptical in any context about the methods of natural science. Let us put the problem another way. Given that a value-free standpoint is arbitrary, but that what we are trying to do is to see whether the social sciences can attain it, is Weber's sociology of politics (unlike Marx's) as value-free as Weber himself maintains?

Weber's sociology of politics centres on his analysis of authority. Weber sees that all political authority rests ultimately on force, but he sees also that this force must be adequately recognized as legitimate for a political system to function at all. According to Weber, there are three fundamental ways whereby this can be effected. The three types of authority exemplifying these three ways are, in Weber's terms, the 'traditional', the 'rational-legal' and the 'charismatic'—this last being a term taken over from its different use in the context of ecclesiastical history. Weber insists that these three are 'ideal types' (or, if you prefer, models); that is to say, they are designed to provide a logical yardstick, not to represent any system existing in historical fact. He does maintain, however, that every political system rests on some combination of these three basic elements.

In Weber's own words, traditional authority rests on 'the general and continuous belief in the sacredness of settled traditions and the legitimacy of the person or persons called to authority by such traditions'—for example, a hereditary tribal chief. Legal authority rests on 'the belief in the legality of a consciously created order and of the right to give commands vested in the person or persons designated by that order'—for example, the elected president of a constitutional republic. Charismatic authority rests on 'the uncommon and extraordinary devotion to the sacredness or the heroic force or the exemplariness of an individual and the order revealed or created by him'—for example, the Mahdi.[1] The crucial difference between charismatic authority and both of the other two is that charismatic authority is inherently unstable. Under a charismatic system, the source and agent of authority are identical, and this means that the durability of the regime is conditional on its continuing success: any failure by the agents of the system is a failure of the system itself, because the actions of the leader and his agents are all that the legitimacy of the system rests on. What is therefore necessary is that the charismatic element should as far as possible be reduced by being transformed into one or other of the traditional and legal types by a process of what Weber calls 'routinization' (*Veralltäglichung*). The threefold typology is offered to us as objective, inclusive and valid for all times and places; but can this claim to a scientific sociology of politics be in practice sustained?

A variety of hostile and sometimes inconsistent criticism has been levelled against Weber on this issue. He has, most obviously and in a sense quite rightly, been accused of anti-Marxist bias. He has also been accused of taking too little account of revolutions (on which he promised but never completed a separate chapter). His typology has been denounced as ahistorical on the grounds that 'not a comprehensive reflection on the nature of political society but merely the experience of two or three generations had supplied the basic orientation'.[2] But, by contrast, it has equally been claimed that his conception of charisma is merely a vehicle for a sort of hero-worshipping, Carlylean philosophy of history.[3] It is, I think, possible to rescue Weber from the more extreme accusations of this type, although this still leaves a number of difficulties (particularly in connection with the 'routinization' of charisma). All that we are here concerned with, however, is whether his typology of authority, whatever its other merits or defects, is as scientific as Weber claims.

Let us take the notion of charisma. Weber claims that charisma is a value-neutral word which can be applied with equal validity to religious leaders or to robber barons provided only that they can be shown empirically to fit the definition. But when Weber talks, as he does, about the 'decline' of charisma, or about priestly charisma being 'degraded' by transformation into political bureaucracy, can we really believe that he is being wholly impartial? Or is he not using his chosen terms in such a way as to give preference to charismatic leaders over bureaucrats? Similarly, when he sees as the result of bureaucratization an increasing emphasis on specialist training rather than the education of the man of all-round culture, and says explicitly that 'The "cultivated man" is here used in a completely value-neutral sense', can we entirely accept the claim? Or is he not loading his definitions just as much as Marx does?

Weber might have several answers to this. He might say that he defines his terms by their meaning to the persons concerned: when, for instance, he talks of 'false' charisma, he means what the followers of the charismatic leader would, if they knew, consider false. Secondly, he might say that although he may have views of his own on these topics, he is quite capable of excluding them from his academic work. Thirdly, he might say that all that matters in any case is whether his conclusions, whatever his initial standpoint, stand up to the objective tests which he himself lays down by value-free criteria. These claims are, I think, tenable up to a point, even if Weber can be shown to depart from them in practice. Even if Weber is a humanist, or a democrat, or an anti-Marxist, or a hero-worshipper, this does not prevent us from testing his conclusions by those rigorous standards which he himself has stipulated; his own views are in principle no more relevant than the religious beliefs which may have prompted an astronomer or a biologist to take up their studies. There is a qualification to Weber's claims to science which does need to be made, but it is a qualification on a slightly different ground.

We have seen that Weber believes, against the extreme positivistic view, that the social sciences differ in kind from the natural. Even leaving aside the problem of the arbitrariness of basic points of view, the uniqueness of historical sequences and the meaningfulness of human behaviour mean that there is a latitude of interpretation always confronting the social scientist which the natural scientist is luckily denied. Weber's procedure in the face of this situation breaks down not because he fails to concede that a sociological inquiry cannot be framed in value-neutral terms, but because this concession does not buy as much immunity from the remaining problems as he thinks. The arbitrariness of standpoints cannot merely be conceded in the original choice of terms, after which, with this sole limitation, the inquiry conducted can be kept value-free. The infection of values cannot all be passed off on to the questions asked and thereby kept away altogether from the answers given. The evaluative terms will have to be used in inquiries within which—and this is my point— no matter how rigorous the techniques of validation applied there will still be some interpretative latitude. I do not mean that Weber is wrong when he says that he uses the term 'cultivated man' without either approval or disapproval, or that he is not entitled to define 'legitimate' as 'considered legitimate by the people concerned'. I mean only that when it comes to an interpretation of the behaviour described, there is more to it than Weber wishes to allow.

It is not enough for the investigator to say that he is neither for charisma nor against it, nor to define charisma in terms of the attitudes to their leaders of the members of the societies described. In explaining a unique historical sequence, to use a word like 'charismatic' is either to impose an evaluation within the investigation itself or, if the term is used only as a tautology, to destroy its explanatory value. It is not merely that Weber does not give (which he does not) adequate criteria for distinguishing a charismatic authority-structure from the other two, particularly from the traditional. The point is that no closed definition of such a term is possible. The most obvious parallel is from jurisprudence: no definition of criminal offences can be devised in advance which will cover all possible cases. This is not simply a matter of evidence. Even when dealing with hypothetical cases where all testimony is assumed to be reliable, it is impossible to give a definition of, say, 'criminal negligence' such that we can deductively infer by reference to the definition whether any given situation fits it. In just the same way, it is not enough for Weber to concede that his initial choice of terms and their definitions is ultimately arbitrary; even after this concession, no historical discussion can be conducted strictly according to the canons of positivistic science.

To emphasize this, however, is not to undermine Weber's valid contention both that testable generalizations are possible in social science and that even particular sociological explanations rest at some point on general pre-

Karl Marx and Max Weber

suppositions of cause and effect. Indeed, it is because he establishes this only after conceding the necessary distinctions between natural and social science that Weber's claims for social science are better tenable, as well as more cautious, than those of the vulgar Marxism which he was concerned to refute. I do not want to argue that Weber was a better historian than Marx, whatever that would mean; but I do want to maintain that as a sociologist of politics he faced up to the problem of 'value-relevance' which Marx, although he had raised it, by-passed. Weber did not succeed in resolving the problem, but he made what must be accounted one of the most rewarding efforts. It remains only to see whether we can find in Weber's political sociology any implications for political philosophy which he was too careful, or too disinterested, or too unaware to make explicit in the way that Marx's political philosophy is explicit.

For convenience, let me remain on the topic of charisma. Where political authority rests principally on charismatic legitimacy—where, that is, the source and agent of authority are identical—then on Weber's analysis it will falter the moment that failure destroys the necessary faith of the subjects in their rulers' personal title to rule. Since in such regimes there is little likelihood of indefinite success, authority is inherently unstable. In bureaucratic or traditional regimes, by contrast, stability is possible precisely because the man can be separated from his office, and it is possible to criticize the actions of an office-holder without thereby criticizing the system by which he holds his office. The difficulty in a charismatic regime is that to criticize even the leader's subordinates is to criticize the system, for the leader and his personal choice of subordinates is all that the system is.

Notice what follows. If, even in a nominally parliamentary or, indeed, hereditary regime, the real basis of authority is in fact charismatic, then the failure of the charismatic leader or body will leave a free-for-all which the remaining political norms may be too weak to resist. Moreover, it may be impossible to allow an effective parliamentary or other opposition without allowing the whole regime to be endangered. When the real source of authority is not in Parliament but in the Head of State in person, then an attack on his ministers in Parliament becomes an attack not only on the ministers but on the system: the opposition must be by definition a disloyal one. Unless, therefore, the basis of authority can be either traditionalized (as it might be, by founding a dynasty) or rationalized (as it might be, by transferring it to the enacted constitution itself), then the regime will remain inherently unstable.

There are, as I have already implied, a lot more difficulties raised by the notion of charisma than Weber himself takes account of. Nor do I propose to try to consider in practice whether France under de Gaulle, Turkey under Ataturk or Ghana under Nkrumah provide the best example of what Weber is talking about. Let us simply suppose that there is in fact a case where Weber's analysis in some sort of useful form applies. Is there not an immediate implication for any political theory which assigns a primary and overriding priority to two-party democracy as the foundation and prerequisite of good government? If this is given a supreme and, as it were, religious value there may be nothing more to be said; but if the advocate of two-party democracy is open to argument at all, then he must in principle be prepared to modify his assertions in the light of just that kind of sociological evidence which Weber's notion of charisma might provide. Once, in a given State, it is shown that there does not exist an adequate basis for either traditional or rational-legal legitimacy, it follows that an attempt to create or live up to a model of two-party parliamentary democracy may endanger the stability of the regime rather than (at this stage, at least) successfully 'routinize' it. A charismatic government may, of course, so behave that its overthrow is morally imperative. But where social conditions are such that—if a Weberian analysis is right—only charismatic authority is workable, then it will not do to object to it on political-philosophical grounds for the sole reason that it is charismatic—or not unless democratic anarchy is held preferable even to the best-administered charismatic authority.

This is not meant as more than a suggestion of how an argument on these lines might run. Nor am I claiming that its most obvious implication—that two-party democracy may not be universally appropriate to emergent nations—is a novel one. It can be claimed that much of what Weber says in discussing charismatic authority is in fact relevant— whether we retain his vocabulary or not—to just these problems. But I am concerned less to argue the issue as such than to suggest that such a large-scale generalization about political authority may not only have a testable content applicable to particular situations but may also have, just as much as Marxism, a direct implication for political theory. Moreover, I have tried to suggest that Weber, by making more cautious claims to science and less ambitious prescriptions for action than the Marxists, shows more clearly—even though his own claims need substantial qualification—the nature of the unavoidable problem of the relation between explanation and evaluation in the social sciences, or between the sociology and the philosophy of politics.

CHAPTER IV

ÉLITES AND OLIGARCHIES

If we owe to Marx and Weber the major preoccupations of political sociology, there is still one important topic that we owe to four very different thinkers of the late nineteenth and early twentieth century. These four, who can be fairly classified as the minor patriarchs of political sociology, are Gaetano Mosca, Vilfredo Pareto, Robert Michels and Georges Sorel. None can be claimed to be of the stature of Marx or Weber. True, Pareto's *Treatise of General Sociology* (translated into English in four volumes as *The Mind and Society*) is a weighty attempt to construct a general sociology of a more or less strictly positivistic kind. But it is an unsuccessful attempt, and the reasons for its failure need not concern us here. The lasting interest of Pareto, as of Mosca, Michels and Sorel, is their contribution to our understanding of what, since Pareto, we refer to as the study of élites; and it is on this topic that these four have earned themselves the convenient but misleading nickname of 'Machiavellians'.

It is, of course, always misleading to lump together any set of similar and more or less contemporary thinkers under a single title. These four, though at some points acknowledging a debt to each other (Michels, for instance, had known Sorel when Sorel was writing the *Reflections on Violence*, and gave explicit credit to both Mosca and Pareto), were also at frequent pains to stress their differences. Thus Mosca vigorously claimed precedence over Pareto in formulating the notion of the political élite; and Sorel, though considered by Pareto merely to have worked out a special case

Élites and Oligarchies

of Pareto's own general theory, is often and rightly claimed to belong to no category but his own. What I shall do, therefore, is to say something separately about Sorel before considering the doctrine of oligarchy more or less common to Mosca, Pareto and Michels.

Sorel was a retired engineer whose intellectual career began only in middle age. Once begun, its apparent inconsistencies are uniquely impressive: Sorel ranged from Marxism to Syndicalism to Monarchism to Leninism to Fascism. However, these bewildering changes of front reflect not an articulated sociology of politics but rather the quest for allies in an unending war against bourgeois decadence. Sorel is, as much as the other three, one of the great *exposeurs* of bourgeois democracy ('democracy', he once said, 'is the paradise of which unscrupulous financiers dream'); but he remains more a moralist than an analyst of politics. He is interesting chiefly as the perpetual outsider of politics, the apostle of a sectarian purity to be maintained in preparation for an apocalyptic struggle which never quite comes. One's political duty, according to Sorel, is to join the dedicated band of revolutionists constantly engaged in reinforcing the solidarity and purpose of the few incorruptibles capable of genuine political action. To Sorel, there is an absolute value in staying always on the outside, in being willing to use a minimum of violence where necessary to carry on the purifying struggle, in exploiting such myths as the 'political general strike' which may focus the revolutionary enthusiasm of the movement. But as a serious political programme, this is clearly self-defeating. Since there is a necessary decadence in belonging to any Establishment, any movement that succeeds is bound to fail. The preservation of the ruthless integrity required for a basically fictitious struggle becomes a sort of running on the spot for the sake of keeping fit, although there will be no serious race to compete in. Sorel's political philosophy is, as it were, a purpose without a goal.

Sorel is important, therefore, neither quite as a philosopher nor quite as a sociologist of politics, and is thus less relevant to my main preoccupation than the other three. He is instead important because he articulates an attitude which can often be basic to sectarian political movements and is therefore basic to our understanding of them. How much he really influenced Mussolini is uncertain; and his admiration for Lenin was not reciprocated.[1] But Sorel, however inconsistent or even ridiculous (as in saying that 'the world will become more just only to the extent that it becomes more chaste'), can help us to understand a certain kind of political feeling in a way that no other author can. In this he is of a totally different kind from Mosca, Pareto and Michels, whose reputation derives rather from their empirical analysis of politics. They have little understanding and less sympathy to spare for the psychotic byways of political enthusiasm; their concern is rather to lay bare the basic facts of political reality. It is by doing this that they have left a more explicit legacy than Sorel to both the sociologists and the philosophers of politics, and must therefore be treated here at greater length. Philosophically, they have forced us to modify the traditional theories of liberal democracy; sociologically, they have bequeathed to us the topic now known as the study (or even theory) of élites.

The usual practice among their commentators is to consider them as political scientists (which indeed they claimed to be) and either to praise them for their clinical scientism or to denounce them for their unconfessed bias. But this does not carry us very much farther, since we already know both that complete scientism is unattainable on these topics and also that it is nevertheless worth trying.

Élites and Oligarchies

What is more interesting is to take the central idea which is more or less shared by all three and to ask—given that it can be stated in a form which is fairly obviously true—what are its implications for traditional political theory? More specifically, what sort of theory of democracy can incorporate the discoveries of Mosca's 'political class', Michels's 'iron law of oligarchy' and Pareto's 'circulation of élites'?

Unfortunately, all three of these ideas are a good deal less precise than their authors seem to have thought them. There is an immediate plausibility about the assertion that oligarchy is inevitable; but is it more than a truism? It can be found not only in Machiavelli but also in Rousseau, who in a single rather startling sentence of *The Social Contract* declares that he knows quite well that democracy is impossible.[1] Clearly, our authors must be trying to say more than this; but just how much more is not made fully apparent in any of their writings.

Here, for instance, is Michels's statement of what he calls 'the fundamental sociological law of political parties': 'It is organization which gives birth to the dominion of the elected over the electors, of the mandatories over the mandators, of the delegates over the delegators. Who says organization, says oligarchy.'[2] But what exactly does this mean? That leaders always try to stay in power? That political organizations can be manipulated? That delegates cannot be effectively bound by the views of their delegators? The 'law', one is tempted to say, is fundamental only by avoiding any attempt to be precise.

If we turn to Mosca, we can likewise find one passage which appears to be giving a cogent formulation of his general claim.[3] 'In all societies,' says Mosca, 'from societies that are very meagrely developed and have barely attained the dawnings of civilization down to the most advanced and powerful societies, two classes of people appear—a class that rules and a class that is ruled. The first class, always the less numerous, performs all political functions, monopolizes power and enjoys the advantages that power brings, whereas the second, the more numerous class, is directly controlled by the first, in a manner that is now more or less legal, now more or less violent, and supplies the first, in appearance at least, with the material means of subsistence and with the instrumentalities that are essential to the vitality of the political organism.' But what, on inspection, does this rather clumsy formulation add up to? We are told that rulers are less numerous than their subjects; that rulers do rule their subjects; and that a ruler is unlikely to bake his own bread or be a member of his own police force. It is, of course, also a reminder in some sense of the realities of power. But is it telling us anything more than Machiavelli and Rousseau?

Thirdly, therefore, we may try to find in Pareto a precise and unambiguous statement about the nature and function of élites. There is in Pareto no single text that stands out quite as the other two do; but several of his general propositions or definitions do seem reasonably clear. The élite, as Pareto defines its membership, is 'those who have the highest indices in their branch of activity'; that is to say (and Pareto is at pains to stress this), those who are best *at* things without any implication that they are thereby or in addition in any moral sense best. The élite is subdivided into the governing and non-governing élite, and there is the further distinction of 'a smaller, choicer class (or else a leader or a committee) that effectively and practically exercises control'. Beyond this, Pareto introduces the notion of the 'circulation' of élites which, whatever the rights and wrongs of his debt to Mosca, is certainly his independent contribution. He did not coin the term any more than Weber coined 'charisma', but it was he who gave it the sense which it has since then borne. Élites, in Pareto's picture, are subject to a constant cycle of decadence and renewal; and those who are qualified for membership of the governing élite are those (in Pareto's own phrase) 'possessing residues suitable for exercising the functions of government and willing enough to use force'.[1] Pareto's term 'residues' we may in this context perfectly well translate as 'qualities', and it accordingly seems fairly clear what Pareto is saying. Moreover, it is also clear that Pareto's notion of the élite need not make him, as his critics sometimes pretend, one of the founding fathers of Fascism.

But once again, does it amount to very much? The Many are again being ruled by the Few; but what else? Different groups gain and lose the position of being the ruling few; but the assertion that they are those whose 'residues' are most suitable is either trivial or false. If the governing élite is defined as the best governors, just as the chess-playing élite is the best chess-players, then to say that the élite will be composed of the best governors is a tautology. If, on the other hand, the élite means those who *happen* to hold what *happen* to be the positions of power, then to say that they are there because they possess the suitable residues is almost certainly untrue. Indeed, in a society where the qualities suitable (whatever that word means) for government are in fact very different from those suitable for getting into the actual position of governing (such as birth, or wealth, or merely sycophancy), then the assertion is quite obviously false. And if Pareto means only that in order to gain power it may help to be skilful and unscrupulous, then once again this is either uninteresting or untrue.

Why, therefore, are Mosca, Pareto and Michels so important to the study of politics? Unless their reputations are grossly inflated, they must be saying more than their central sociological propositions, taken in isolation, would suggest. These central propositions amount to little more than that all governments are oligarchies; and, in fact, the principal reason for the influence of all three authors is the impact of their writings not as systematic treatises but as exposés. All three are saying—but with less heat and more evidence than Sorel—that democracy is a fraud. The fashionable theories of power in the hands of the people and the practices claimed to embody the people's will make no difference whatever to the unalterable realities of power. The form of government is immaterial, for it will never undo these realities: government is always by (and, largely, for) the few. This strenuous reminder of oligarchy, though it may be only restating what has been said by others elsewhere, acquires a different and more powerful significance when seen against a background of purportedly democratic institutions and practices. The constitutional and organizational forms which all three authors discuss are the expression of expectations founded precisely upon the belief that democracy can be put into practice. To denounce this burgeoning orthodoxy, therefore, is to take up a position both provocative and original. To say that all previous governments have been oligarchies is interesting if not profound; to say that democratic governments are and always will be is startling.

For this reason, Michels is the most cogent of the three, although he is much the least original. His attack on those political parties whose principles are most flagrantly contradicted by their practices is in some ways the sharpest of the oligarchic jabs into the complacency of democratic platitudes. It is true that not even the focus on parties is original to Michels, for Ostrogorski's study had already put forward a similar thesis: 'government', says Ostrogorski, 'is a monopoly; it is in the hands of a class which, without forming a caste, constitutes a distinct group in society'; and again, 'a highly developed electoral system is therefore only a purely formal homage to democracy, and produces, in reality, a diminution of its strength'.[1] Ostrogorski, however, goes on to make the fantasy proposal of the abolition of permanent parties, and his conclusions are much less incisive than those of Michels. Michels (and Mosca and Pareto) wanted not only to show, as Ostrogorski did, that something was going wrong with democracy in practice; they wanted also to show that it could never go right.

Of the three, Pareto's language is most explicitly that of the ruthless iconoclast of illusions. He is always talking about masks being torn away or people being led by the nose. Indeed, the whole of *The Mind and Society* (which contains such bizarre tit-bits as anecdotes of the medieval prosecutions of leeches for trespass) may be seen as no more than a massive assault on the folly of human self-deception. But all three authors wrote to some degree in the light of a personal disillusionment. Michels as a young man had sacrificed the advantages of a bourgeois upbringing for his Socialist sympathies. Mosca, who grew up in the hopeful years of Italy's early independence, witnessed the steady and painful awakenings of the 1880's and 1890's, and indeed had already been exposed, before moving to Rome in his late twenties, to the disillusioning workings of Sicilian politics. Pareto, though of the three he had least contact with actual political life, was embittered by the rejection of the free-trade policies which he had supported in the 1880's with all the weight of his academic reputation. In the work of all three, and most of all in Pareto, there is the tone of injured innocence, of the pained recognition of ugly facts. All three write as though firmly resolved to strip away the pretensions by which others might still be deceived.

There is of course more than this in the work of all three. But in the further ramifications of their argument, however interesting, they tend to weaken their central case rather than strengthen it. One of Michels's points, for instance, is that the leaders of proletarian movements are always middle-class. But although this may be so—Michels even states it elsewhere as a 'historical law'[1]—it has really nothing to do with oligarchy. It merely obscures Michels's central thesis and gives his opponents (such, for instance, as Lukacs) the chance to appear to controvert that thesis if they can show that proletarian parties need not in fact be bourgeois-led. The same sort of diffusion of argument weakens the work of Pareto and Mosca. A great deal of Pareto's *Systèmes Socialistes* (published in 1902 but still unavailable in English) is taken up with the strenuous thumping of very straw men. The wilder fantasies of such Utopian Communists as Cabet or Fourier, who pictured a world of harnessed whales and seas of lemonade, are too easy a target for a broadside against them to carry much conviction. *The Mind and Society* is largely taken up, as I have mentioned, with denouncing human irrationalities. But however entertaining or peculiar these may be, they are merely distractions from a very inadequate psychology and a sociology of politics which is a good deal less rigorous than it pretends. Mosca, likewise, fails adequately to relate his notions of history and society to his theory of the ruling class. It is not that many other of his ideas are not exceedingly interesting—for instance, his contention that a standing

Élites and Oligarchies

army will be a guarantee of political freedom. But they need always to be systematically disentangled from the discussion of the inevitability of oligarchy.

Once, however, the necessary disentanglements have been made and we have unravelled the semblance, however fragile, of a 'theory' of oligarchy, an obvious comparison springs to mind. What Pareto or Sorel at their most abusive have to say about bourgeois democracy is not very different from what is said by Marx. Pareto explicitly describes the Marxian theory of class as 'une idée très nette', and one of Sorel's most pungent essays is on the 'decomposition' (which he deplores) of Marxism. Is not Pareto's 'governing élite' simply another name for Marx's capitalist class? With reservations, the answer can be made a yes; but the two major reservations are enough to show how little of a Marxist can really be made of Pareto. In the first place, Pareto does not believe, as Marx does, that the basis of all political power is economic; and in the second he altogether rejects the notion that oligarchy will only persist until the successful transition to Communism from the dictatorship of the proletariat. Pareto's commentators rightly point out that he only approves of Marx to the extent that he can stand him on his head. But the comparison of Marx and Pareto makes two further conclusions clear. First, Marx's classes and Pareto's élites must at some point be involved in the explanation of each other; second, there are many more questions about the nature of the power of the governing élite than either Marx or Pareto seem to have asked themselves.

Marx in a sense does better on this second topic, because he has a very clear, if circumscribed, idea of how the bourgeois élite (or capitalist class) operates. Even if his analysis leaves some questions unanswered, it comes much nearer to a full-fledged theory than anyone else has done on these topics. Mosca, Michels and even Pareto are all three much vaguer than Marx, no matter what allowances we try to make for them. However interesting, Mosca's 'juridical defence', Michels's 'cult of veneration among the masses' and Pareto's cycle of rising and decadent élites all leave unanswered the most sociologically important questions about the holders of power. Is that power economic, or judicial, or military, or even spiritual? Does the governing élite, however defined, share the same qualifications, or attitudes, or neither? How far and at what points is its power limited, and by what or whom? Is it cohesive and stable, or diffuse and factional? And so on. None of these questions is really tackled by our authors. All that we can look to them for is the earnest reminder, however passionlessly they pretend to phrase it, that oligarchy is inevitable and therefore democracy either a will-o'-the-wisp or a sham.

The best line to follow from them, therefore, is to take some general form of their central argument as given. Let us say simply, without feeling a need to pose as impassive clinicians of political change, that even democratic government is in some sense government by the few and that this is bound to be worrying to anyone concerned to preserve or to maximize the redress of the citizen body against despotism. Can we do anything, in the face of the oligarchic reminder, to set this worry at rest?

In terms of political philosophy, the answer to this question will of course be of no great interest to those for whom the problem has already been decided on other grounds. Those who put an absolute value on aims which can only be realized by authoritarian means will be simply indifferent to the problem of maximizing the liberty (in the

Élites and Oligarchies

Western liberal sense) of the citizen body, just as the religious believer (as it were) in a one- or two-party system will remain unconvinced by sociological arguments to the effect that a different system of parties may be an occasional necessity for the furtherance of his professed objectives. If, however, such underlying beliefs are capable of being argued at all, then this sort of sociological evidence will be the most relevant to the argument. In fact, the argument to which the sociology of élites[1] is most directly relevant is one of the oldest and hardiest arguments in traditional political theory: how should the subject be guaranteed against the State?

One answer sometimes given is that the governing élite should in a strict sense be 'representative' of the governed mass. This is the proposal put forward, for instance, by Professor Duverger at the conclusion of his skilful and comprehensive study of *Political Parties*. 'The formula "Government of the people by the people"', says Duverger, 'must be replaced by this formula: "Government of the people *by an élite sprung from the people*".'[2] It is hard to see, however, that this is anything to do with it. A proletarian élite may be no more likely than a bourgeois élite to guarantee the liberty of the individual citizen; indeed, Duverger himself sometimes implies that on occasion it may be less so. Of course there is a certain appeal in the argument that representative democracy should be truly representative—that is, that the élite should not be drawn only from a single profession, or age-group or economic class. Similarly, there is an appeal in Michels's accusation of hypocrisy against so-called proletarian parties which are bourgeois-led. But the conclusion that should be drawn from such arguments is not that a greater 'representativeness' in this sense will provide a guaranteed restraint on oligarchic despotism. Not only is there no necessary reason why such restraints will be guaranteed simply by mirroring in the governing élite the social characteristics of the people; but if the argument is pressed to its conclusion, it is likely that the contrary will be the case. The average characteristics of the population will not on any analysis be what Pareto would call the residues suitable for government; and unless we believe that a particular social characteristic is necessarily correlated with the virtues we should like to see realized in our rulers, then there is no argument for saying that as a matter of principle rulers must, as a body, statistically reflect the attributes of those whom they rule. The representativeness argument, as we shall see in a moment, must be interpreted in a wholly different sense of the word 'represent'.

A different answer to the question is that provided by Schumpeter. Schumpeter's analysis (as put forward in *Capitalism, Socialism and Democracy*) not only implies a cogent recommendation but rests on one of the shrewdest analyses of Western 'democratic' politics since Mosca, Pareto and Michels themselves. His conclusion, in a sentence as caustic as anything said by Michels, is that 'democracy is the rule of the politician'.[1] It is not, according to Schumpeter, the electorate by whom issues are decided, but rather the leaders and would-be leaders who are required to compete for the electorate's votes. The democratic method is in Schumpeter's definition 'that institutional arrangement for arriving at political decisions in which individuals acquire the power to decide by means of a competitive struggle for the people's vote'. Two implications follow from this. First, the analogy with capitalism is close enough to suggest (which Schumpeter does) that it is unlikely to be a historical accident: what we understand as 'democracy' (i.e., 'liberal' or 'bourgeois' democracy) may under different historical

Élites and Oligarchies

conditions not be the only necessary or even workable way of running a modern industrial society. But secondly, the mutual implication between democracy and freedom which is axiomatic to the European political tradition may perhaps be better explained by Schumpeter's analysis than by classical democratic theory. Since the essence of liberal democracy is that different aspirants to the governing élite must enter into free competition for electoral choice, may not this be the essential means by which liberal democracy guarantees its citizens against despotism?

Again, the answer is, unfortunately, 'not quite'. The lack of choices open to an electorate under a one-party system is to Western democrats a sufficient demonstration that such systems involve the basic denial of political liberty. But choices can, after all, be exercised under such systems, even if at a different level and in a different way; and free competition can be shown in any case not to be the answer. Free competition is no guarantee against either monopolies, or price-rigging, or unethical practices. Hitler, it is worth remembering, came to power by entirely constitutional means. The virtue of the liberal democratic system as it is analysed by Schumpeter is not so much that competition between élites is a sufficient condition of liberty as that such competition may be one way of attaining a necessary condition of liberty: namely, that the governing élite may always be liable to be sacked.

There are, in fact, two and only two general principles which can be laid down for the defence of the citizen body against its oligarchs. Neither is new. Both are universally applicable, however democratic the system (and whatever that word should be taken to mean). Moreover, they embody the basis of good sense which underlies both the representativeness and the competition arguments. The first is that the governing élite must somehow be replaceable by those whose interests (not whose characteristics) it 'represents'. The second is that the governing élite must be adequately diffused. The first is at least as old as the practice of ostracism in ancient Athens; the second is at least as old as Polybius's analysis of the Roman constitution and the doctrine of the separation of powers.

The two principles are not wholly separate, for to be replaceable an élite will have to be accessible and to be accessible it will have to be diffused. But let us look first of all at the question of replaceability. The danger is not merely the self-perpetuation of a closed élite such as is castigated by Michels. Even with as well-intentioned an oligarchy as one could choose, there is the further problem of information: the Few have to realize what the Many want and the Many have to have some means of finding out whether the Few are really giving it to them. It is here that the representativeness argument is relevant, for if the rights of the citizen body (and particularly the minority groups within it) are to be maintained, then their interests must be 'represented' in the different sense of that word from the social composition argument of Professor Duverger. This does not mean necessarily that the governing élite should include members of all the different social groups or classes, though this may in practice be a useful way of achieving the desired result. What it does mean is that it must always be possible to appoint into the élite (and to influence after appointment) some person or persons who will defend the interests of those whom they represent and who may be replaced if they fail to do so. For this purpose, the élite must not only be open; it must also, in practice, be decentralized. It is not enough to say that rulers must be accessible to scrutiny; they must be accessible at as many points as is administratively workable.

Élites and Oligarchies

The argument is familiar. If the various areas of governmental power are concentrated into the same hands, then this power can be more readily abused; but if different persons are more or less independently responsible for different areas—fiscal and military, legislative and executive, or whatever it may be—then they are more likely to have to exercise their power in the common interest. This is, in effect, the 'checks and balances' argument of the traditional constitutional theorists. In another form, it is part of the liberal argument for pluralism against the monolithic élites of the authoritarian societies. But it is in principle applicable in any form of society where oligarchies rule—and that is to say, if we believe Michels and the others, in any form of society. Élites must not too much overlap if they are not to have more power than is likely to be comfortable for everyone else.

But where do these platitudes lead us? They are easy enough in theory, whether put forward by traditional constitutional philosophers or modern political scientists; but applied to the complexities of practical government, do they say anything interesting or new? This sort of doubt, by which theorists of politics must always (and perhaps rightly) be disturbed, is particularly cogent on just these topics. Not only is the concept of power, which is what we are fundamentally concerned with, extraordinarily difficult and elusive in itself; but it is in practice very hard to collect adequate evidence for forming general conclusions about it. No satisfactory definition of power has yet been produced, although both philosophers and political scientists have attempted to do so. But even if it had, the topic is still one which is more appropriate to the traditional methods of the historian than to any statistical index devised by the wizards of political science. It is seldom easy in a given society or even organization to find out who are the actual holders of power—who, that is to say, is under normal conditions empowered to decide and enforce what. It is almost impossible to say who has more or less power than who else. The meaning to be given to the question is uncertain; but even if stated as concretely as 'who could sack whom?' the answer depends on circumstances which may never arise, which if they do will be unique to the particular historical occasion, and which will in any case be almost certainly inaccessible at several points even to the most dogged academic researcher. This places a major restraint on the ambitions of scientists of politics. But despite all such reservations, there are still two general morals which the theorist may draw from the fact of universal oligarchy and the precautions which suggest themselves against it.

If we start from the assumption that there is in some form an iron law of oligarchy, and if we conclude that the two most important questions which it raises for the would-be democrat are the replaceability and diffusion of the governing élite, then it follows that we should think of revising some of the better-worn criteria for the appraisal of political systems. If 'democratic government' in some non-authoritarian sense which can be broadly agreed upon depends in large part on these two factors, then such questions as the relative merits of one or many parties, presidential or parliamentary constitutions, and so on, are interesting chiefly to the extent that these are the factors affecting the replaceability and diffusion of the governing élite. Of course, if we alter the assumption of political freedom as implicit in the definition of democratic government, then the programme of the argument is altered accordingly. If the aim is, as in a totalitarian system, to reduce rather than to enlarge the areas of social life in which the citizen acts only (in Rousseau's sense) as man, then a closed and centralized élite becomes an obvious means whereby this goal may be more effectively pursued. But even here, the mechanisms of replacement will be crucial. It may be desirable, as was actually done in Soviet Russia during the height of Stalinism, literally to rejuvenate the governing élite by replacing the older members with new. Replacement of this kind will be a problem under any system, authoritarian or democratic; there are as few constitutional bulwarks that can be built in against gerontocracy as against oligarchy, for the principle of election is never by itself sufficient, as mass democracy has in practice made clear. Under any system of government—even where individual liberty is being sacrificed by either necessity or design—efficiency requires that those members of the élite may be replaced who have failed to further the interests of those of the governed on whose support or acquiescence any government ultimately rests.

What we must ask, therefore, is not 'how many offices are elective?' or 'how many proletarians hold Cabinet office?' or even 'what democratic guarantees are written into the constitution?'. Machine politics has shown that, for instance, an elective judiciary may give rise to the opposite of its ostensible purpose; the history of the British Labour Party and of a number of trade unions provides adequate evidence to show that proletarians in office may turn out less radical than many of their bourgeois colleagues; and constitutions, as Stalin's Russia amply demonstrates, can in practice mean nothing at all. We must instead ask such questions as 'under what circumstances can the effective leaders be replaced?', 'who can influence the decisions taken by the effective leaders?' and 'how accessible are the effective leaders to accurate information about the felt wants of the governed?'.

This change of emphasis leads directly to the second point. The reminder that even democracies are oligarchies requires us to assess the practical workings of democracy by rather different criteria from those envisaged by its earlier proponents; and the questions now seen to be relevant make clear that we must also revise our traditional theories of political participation. The old democratic model was of participation through the suffrage in decisions affecting the communal welfare. But the fact of oligarchy makes this in practice something of a myth. Moreover, the tendency to oligarchy has been yet further accentuated by the complexity and, above all, size of the great majority of nation-states. Even Rousseau—once again—was aware of the crucial effect of size on the possibility of democratic government. The result is that the effective representation of articulate, shared interests takes place not so much through the ballot-box as through the rather different agency of what we now refer to as pressure-groups.

Pressure-groups are not new, of course. In fact, they are very old indeed if so defined as to include not only all trade unions, but the anti-slavery movement and even the Law Society, which is now over two hundred years old. But their expansion in size and importance is very recent, and so is the interest of political scientists in them, particularly in Great Britain. Only in the last few years have academic studies been carried out on such diverse bodies as the British Medical Association, the National Farmers Union and the group of backbench Conservative M.P.'s responsible, we are told, for the successful introduction into Great Britain of commercial television. Pressure-groups, says Mr J. D. Stewart in his study of their relation to the House of Commons, 'have become a fifth estate'.[1] Whether or not we agree entirely with Schumpeter that it is politicians and

Élites and Oligarchies

not voters by whom issues are decided—and the case of commercial television in Britain appears to offer an example of just this claim—it is still through the lobby rather than the vote that oligarchy is best influenced in practice. It is therefore here, where coherent sectional interests have access to the governing élite, that we must look if we are to construct or appraise a theory of democracy that takes account of Mosca, Pareto and Michels.

Unfortunately, democracy of the lobby has not yet found its philosopher, as democracy of the ballot-box did in Bentham and the Mills. We know an increasing amount about the actual workings of pressure-group politics, and we are more or less used to the idea that governmental decisions are, as Professor Dahl says of the United States, made by 'endless bargaining', the product of 'the steady appeasement of relatively small groups'.[1] But what are the general theoretical principles by which such bargaining should be governed? Are pressure-groups in our society allowed too much influence or too little? Should they be seen as enabling an organized minority to impose its interests against those of the nation at large, or as affording representation to interests whose organization has earned them the right to be heard? Is it perhaps in the extension of influence of articulate, competitive interests, not in the simple separation of governmental powers, that the metaphor of 'checks and balances' is most appropriate? Could it be by the multiplication of pressure-groups that the accessibility and diffusion of the governing élite may be most beneficially achieved?

The theoretical problems raised by such questions as these are still awaiting an answer. In nineteenth-century Britain, as David Butler has reminded us,[2] the word 'reform', when used in a political context, denoted electoral reform; in the twentieth century it does not. The dissatisfied democrat can no longer put forward as a panacea the simple extension of democracy interpreted in terms of the franchise. The dangers of oligarchy have outlasted the advent of universal suffrage as Mosca, Pareto and Michels were right to discern that they were doing. The lobby, therefore, has become the focus both for access by the governed to the oligarchs but also for pressure on the oligarchs by unrepresentative minorities of the governed. We know an increasing amount about how these pressures work. But a theory of democracy laying down principles for their regulation has yet to be formulated.

One kind of answer may seem to be provided by the totalitarian states, in which pluralism is on principle denounced, however much pressure-groups may continue to operate within the framework of the one-party structure. But it is worth remarking that even in those countries where the governing élite is least accessible and most highly centralized, this is not taken to involve a denial of the principle that government should give expression to the needs and wishes of the governed. It is instead claimed first, that interests are best articulated within the unitary political system, not from outside it; and second, that a national emergency, whether created from within or without, is the justification for a closed and centralized élite which would readily be more liberal if only circumstances would permit. It is not, therefore, that Western pluralism affirms that governments should be as accessible as possible to the popular will while totalitarian democracy rejects it. Both systems claim to recognize and to implement the popular will, and both are prepared to curtail the liberties implied by that principle when war or conspiracy seems to demand it. The differences between the two systems are indeed enormous, but they do not involve two rival theories of the legitimacy of pressure-groups so much as two rival theories of political participation. The lobbies at work in the different systems are required to work under very different conditions of freedom of organization and expression. But the principles as well as the problems of giving weight to competing claims are common to both. There are two very different theories of how the popular will is to be reflected in the electoral choice by the people of their rulers; but how rulers, once in power, are to adjudicate the claims of conflicting sectional interests is a problem which seems to be dealt with in no less unsystematic a manner in totalitarian than in liberal democracies.

It may be that in fact there are no comprehensive principles which could be put forward by a self-styled philosopher of pressure-groups. It may be that here, above all, politics is really 'the art of the possible', and nothing further can be said about it than this. But the problem is a real one, and one which was largely by-passed by the traditional emphasis on how rulers were to be appointed rather than how they should or should not be influenced once in power. Perhaps, indeed, it has been economics rather than politics which has been more concerned with the theoretical issues involved, for the problems of welfare economics, bargaining disputes and the aggregation of utility preferences all bear directly on the question of how the 'popular will' can in practice be best given expression. It cannot, perhaps, be claimed that welfare economics has solved or even looks likely to solve the perennial difficulties raised by competing preferences. But for just this reason, the issue is one which well illustrates the general thesis of these essays: if there is to be any solution to the most important questions of contemporary politics, neither the philosophers nor the social scientists, of whatever kind, are likely to get on very well without each other. This applies both to the problem of how oligarchies (that is, governments) should respond to sectional interests and also to how the members of oligarchies should be selected by those they claim to represent. It is this second topic which will be the theme of the following chapter.

CHAPTER V

VOTERS AND PARTIES

The rediscovery—whether a paradox or a truism—that even democracies are oligarchies should not, of course, be taken too far. I tried to suggest in the last chapter why it is important to the theorist or philosopher of democracy, but this need not imply that all our national elections are merely a predetermined shadow-play enacted according to the oligarchs' whim. Even on Schumpeter's analysis, which would probably be agreed by most political scientists to underestimate the role of the electorate, it is the electorate who choose (subject to manipulation) which of the competing oligarchies is to decide for them. We must still look at the political process as a reciprocal interaction between governors and governed; and in fact it is the study of the governed, in their role of electorate, that has been one of the most fruitful for political scientists (or sociologists) during the last few decades. The development of sample survey techniques and their application to the mass electorate have yielded a quantity of information which, however it should be interpreted, was simply not available to the political theorist or historian of before the Second World War. We must ask, therefore, the same two questions which run through all of these essays: first, how 'scientific' are the conclusions which the sociologists of politics have made available to us? and second, what do these conclusions imply for political theory?

I do not mean, however, that the new techniques of studying voting behaviour have in any sense replaced the more traditional studies of the electorate. The study of electorates is of course largely concerned with the actual voting decision and its outcome in the aggregate at a given election. But this is far from the whole of it. An understanding of the electorate involves not only detecting what really happens at the ballot-box, but also the analysis of the constitutional regulations, party structures and the whole political system within which a given election takes place. This makes clear that any debate about quantitative versus non-quantitative methods is, as usual, misconceived. Votes, which have the great advantage of being a countable as well as a significant political act, are highly suitable for statistical techniques; indeed psephology, so-called, would obviously get nowhere at all without them. On the other hand, the assessment of what, say, would have happened if the Prime Minister had adopted a different policy or held a given election at a different date is equally obviously quite impervious to statistical reduction. An understanding of the British general elections of the 1950's is incomplete, however carefully the electorate is interviewed and the voting figures analysed, without an understanding which only the historian can provide of the twentieth-century background of British politics. I make this obvious assertion only because I shall be discussing non-historical methods, and I had better therefore stress that by so doing I am not implying that they are substitutes for political history. They are adjuncts which, however useful, can only answer the questions to which they are appropriate.

The principal change which these newer methods have effected has been to revise the traditional picture of the 'rational' voter. Of course, long before the development of the systematic interview, observers of politics had cast strong doubts on the rationality of the electorate. Ostrogorski, whom we have already met as a sceptic of democracy, was one of these. So was Graham Wallas, whose *Human Nature in Politics* (1908) is still a powerful, if old-fashioned, assault on what Wallas called the tendency to 'exaggerate the intellectuality of mankind'. But by and large it was assumed throughout the first few decades of this century that what the electorate does is to make a deliberate choice between two (or more) alternatives as presented to it during the election campaign. What it has been surprising to discover is just how far the voters for the different parties are 'predisposed' to vote the way that they do long before the start of the campaign. Voting, in fact, seems a good deal less of a decision than of a habit.

This finding has now become a commonplace. But the history of the landmark study, Lazarsfeld's *The People's Choice*, is itself the best testimony to that study's originality. So far were the investigators' findings from what they expected that they at one point laid aside their data for a year—purely, it appears, as a result of their disappointment with their first tabulations.[1] The study, though not published until 1944, is of a sample of the electorate of Erie County, New York, during the presidential election of 1940. Lazarsfeld, who had been a pioneer of market and mass media research in the 1930's, seems to have started by supposing the voting decision to be a sort of individual choice like the choice of two alternative products in a department store. It turned out instead that a voter's choice could be largely predicted from two or three social characteristics; that those most influenced by the campaign were not the mythical 'floating vote' but those already most partisan; and that voters were moved more by the urge to conform to their social group than to express an articulated political decision. All these conclusions were, of course, tentative. Not only was it the first study of its kind, but its implications might, after all, apply only to the place and time at which it was conducted. Moreover, there were a number of deficiencies in the technical design of the study, as its authors readily admitted. But their conclusions, however debatable the interpretation to be placed on them, have been largely confirmed by their successors. Although imperfections or limitations of a technical kind, as well as inconsistencies of terminology, can be pointed out in all of the voting studies carried out in Britain and the United States since *The People's Choice*, their actual findings remain the best evidence we have for what sort of person votes how. The more difficult problem is whether learning how people vote can also tell us why.[1]

The basic issues have been to some extent obscured by the emphasis on successful prediction of specific election results. Given adequate sampling, a British or American national election is predictable to within a few per cent, even though this may be—as most notoriously in the American presidential election of 1948—too broad a margin to yield the actual result. The principal correlates of voting behaviour are sufficiently well established for such predictions to have been reduced to a progressively more accurate routine. The sample design must be good, the interval between interview and prediction not too long, and certain standard manipulations of the results must be made to allow for those likely to express an opinion without actually reaching the ballot-box. With such precautions as these, we can at worst make a much better guess about the outcome of elections than anyone could do before the days of the sample survey. But what this emphasis on prediction obscures is that the political sociologist is concerned less with prediction than with diagnosis.

Of course, the test of a diagnosis is likely to be a prediction. But, as I have already argued in chapter 1, a diagnosis will not be falsified if the conditions under which it is claimed to apply are not in fact fulfilled. If I say, for instance, that rising prosperity will cause a higher proportion of young manual workers to vote Conservative than hitherto, my assertion is not controverted if they fail to vote Conservative at an election held during a slump which started only after I said what I did. It is also true, of course, that my diagnosis has not been confirmed, for to establish under what conditions and to what extent my generalization will hold good I have to be able to observe a situation where the specific conditions are realized. But to say that an explanation of voting behaviour is wrong because a prediction made by its author is incorrect may not be necessarily true. This refutation would only follow if the election were held under the conditions of a controlled experiment.

There is another point also. Predictions, on the natural science model, are based on observed correlations. Applied to voting behaviour, this means for example that if urban Catholics have an observed statistical tendency to vote Democrat in a higher proportion than non-Catholics (even at the same level of income), then this will be incorporated into the prediction about the given electorate on the basis of the proportion of such potential voters that it contains. But even if this prediction turns out to be entirely correct—as American experience suggests it will—it does not thereby establish the proposition that being a Catholic 'causes' a given social category to vote Democrat in a higher proportion. Nor is this because the correlation might be a statistical accident, such as in controlled experiments can be guarded against by an appropriate test of statistical significance. It is because, in the social sciences, correlation can never by itself constitute an adequate demonstration of cause. The behaviour being studied is the result of conscious and meaningful action by the persons concerned; and although non-correlation may be enough to refute our interpretation of their behaviour, the converse does not at all apply.[1] Our assertion of cause and effect in human behaviour depends in addition on certain intuitive notions which are not derived simply from observation of correlations. Suppose, for instance, that as good a correlation is observed between voting Labour and having red hair as between voting Labour and being an industrial worker. It would surely be difficult to take seriously anyone who claimed that the first correlation was as likely to be a causal relation as the second.

For these reasons, we must be very careful about the jump from prediction to explanation. The voting studies have described to us much better than could be done before many of the characteristics correlated with voting in a certain way. But the jump to explanations is still questionable. Given that being a Catholic correlates with being a Democrat, the question 'why?' is not so much answered as asked. It may be, for instance, that being Catholic and being Democrat are both correlated with some other fact which is the cause of both—being an immigrant into the United States is one cause which has been suggested for this. Or it may be that the correlation of Catholics and Democrats is a hangover from 1928, when the Democratic candidate was for the first time a Catholic. Or it may be that some common psychological influence helps to predispose a man to be both a Catholic and a Democrat. What the investigator has to decide, and cannot decide on strictly positivistic criteria, is which correlation to follow up. In doing this—both in

Voters and Parties

deciding and in following up his decision—he will act a good deal more like a historian than a natural scientist.

There have been broadly two different sorts of correlation on which the two schools of American voting studies have focused their attention: the more social and the more psychological. Lazarsfeld and his successors at Columbia University have, as we saw, been principally concerned with such suggested influences on the voter as his social group (in the sense of family, friends and 'opinion leaders'), and his broader social characteristics (religion, urban or rural residence and 'socio-economic status'). The series of studies conducted by the Survey Research Centre of the University of Michigan have, on the other hand, concentrated on what their authors have called the 'attitudinal approach'; that is to say, on such more immediate psychological motives as 'issue partisanship' or identification with one or other political party. Both types of correlation have produced consistent accounts of the behaviour of voters. But, as we have seen, it does not follow from this that the proper questions have been asked in terms of an explanation of this behaviour. Of the two, the social approach is likely to be the more useful, for it produces more of the evidence on which a final historical or psychological explanation would have to be based. The 'attitudinal' approach, by contrast, runs grave risk of going round in circles. To say that a man voted for Stevenson in 1952 or 1956 because of his Democratic affiliation says virtually nothing. To say (which must be possible if the first assertion was not a tautology) that he voted for Eisenhower in spite of his Democratic affiliation is to raise the interesting question without answering it; and to say that he did so because his 'candidate partisanship' was stronger is only to go round in circles again.[1] The answers needed are to a different sort of question—the sort of question, in fact, which would be asked by a historian.

To say that a man voted for Eisenhower because he liked him, or that a Democrat voted for Stevenson because he was a Democrat, is not even to take the search for explanation back one more stage. The question 'why?' remains as little answered, and the first step in taking it farther is to ask what other characteristics which might (intuitively) be thought relevant are common to those Democrats who did not vote for Stevenson rather than to those who did. Indeed, it is the examination of the so-called 'deviant cases' which is likely to be most suggestive. There is nothing, in a sense, that needs to be explained about a South Wales miner voting Labour or an executive of General Motors voting Republican. The simplest model of rational self-interest is enough to explain these cases without, in defiance of Graham Wallas, exaggerating the 'intellectuality' involved. The question 'why?' can still be asked, of course, as it always can indefinitely. But it turns at this point into a historical question about how the Labour Party came to represent the working-class interest. It could be answered by an account of how the 'Lib-Lab' miners' M.P.'s of the early years of this century decided to affiliate with the newly formed Labour Party, how the Conservative Party behaved on the mines question after the First World War, and so on. To ask for a further or deeper psychological explanation would be like calling in an analyst to explain why a child wishes to eat when it is hungry. A further explanation is called for only when the pattern becomes less simple: when, for instance, one member in three of the British working class votes Conservative (which they do), or when a conflict of characteristics and opinions (Lazarsfeld's 'cross-pressures') makes it difficult to see what determines the final choice.

Voters and Parties

The 'crucial' factor in such doubtful cases is virtually impossible to determine. Even given a controlled experiment, it would be impossible to be sure: a man might make his decision for some anomalous and even arbitrary reason (such as liking the candidate's name) and not for the final variable isolated by the patient experimenter. The best that can be done is to try to isolate the broad predispositions which seem to be shared by a given category of voter. These may be either psychological (such as in the suggestion that those with a common kind of paternal upbringing shared an impulse to vote for Eisenhower), or social (such as in suggesting that ethnic minorities will vote for what they see as the underdog party). In either case, the best that the survey researcher can do is to collect as much information that may be causally relevant as he can. The choice of possible interpretations (which I shall return to in chapter VI) depends on criteria external to the correlations detected and the predictions thereby made.

There are thus many questions we cannot yet (if ever) hope to answer about the precise causes and effects, under different conditions, of the multifarious factors which may modify the voters' choice. But we do know a good deal more than we used to, even if the selection of causes remains an open one. Surveys have now been carried out in many countries of the world, as well as Great Britain and the United States, which provide evidence from which descriptive generalizations can be made and causal hypotheses defended (if never finally proved). Some of the observed correlations, indeed, were detected well before the heyday of the sample survey. André Siegfried, who carried out a pioneer study in electoral geography in France before the First World War, seems to have been the first person to point out the radicalism of fishermen[1]—a finding which has been borne out in a sufficient number of countries at a sufficient number of times to suggest that there is some general predisposition irrespective of nationality.

But again, the correlation only raises the question: why? According to one theory, it is because fishermen are in an occupation where they are not so much poor as liable to cyclical fluctuations of poverty and prosperity; this interpretation may be perhaps supported by a similar tendency to radicalism among occupational groups as diverse as Swedish lumbermen and Australian sheepshearers. On the other hand, there is an alternative theory according to which it is the social isolation of such occupations which predisposes those in them to radicalism; there is a great deal of evidence to show, for instance, that the larger a factory, and the less social contact its workers therefore have with members of the clerical or managerial class, the more radical they are likely to be. Both are debatable, but both are probably partly true. In choosing between such suggestions, we can only plod along by intuitive plausibility and what Mill called the 'method of residues'— holding as many factors in common as possible and seeing what remains. Unfortunately, as Mill was fully aware, it is seldom or never that historical situations are as directly comparable as this requires; and, as we have seen, all that such comparisons can in any case do is to refute some of our suggestions. We may discover that fishermen are radical even when their incomes are secure; but this will not prove to us which other possible causes are really at work. We still have to keep on sampling successive populations of fishermen under successive (and therefore different) historical conditions.

But this interminability of the question why voters vote as they do does not diminish the fact that we now know far more about *how* they vote than Madison, or Bagehot, or Bryce or even Ostrogorski and Michels. The question which this poses for the political theorist is—as with the rediscovery of oligarchy—whether democracy is after all quite so splendid an ideal as its early proponents and philosophers tended to argue. Since the modern voting studies have begun to appear, the case has been argued with some energy but as yet no very great conclusiveness. The argument chiefly centres on what is seen as the startling apathy of the electorate. Not only do relatively few people change their vote during a campaign or even between one election and the next, but voters are largely ill-informed and even uninterested about the issues which they are supposed to decide. This is an evident divergence from the traditional model of democratic participation, quite apart from the divergence involved in the oligarchic machinations documented by Michels. Even if Schumpeter is wrong, and the electorate is not quite so much the dependent half of the political process, can the disclosure of apathy be kept consistent with what democracy is traditionally supposed to achieve?

The anti-democratic arguments are obvious: the prejudice, ignorance and indifference apparently revealed in the voting studies seem more than enough to justify the criticisms voiced by the aristocratic opponents of mass society, or the misgivings ventured earlier by Tocqueville and Mill. But a number of counter-arguments are offered by the electorate's defenders. In the first place, it may be disputed that what the electorate is required to do is to voice decisions on issues, as opposed to broad preferences of party; secondly, it is claimed that the stability of the electorate, which the voting studies as well as other electoral analyses have demonstrated, is evidence that individual prejudices are not incompatible with collective good sense; and thirdly, it is argued that such apathy or prejudice can in any case be justified by the beneficial results which they in fact engender for the democratic system. This third argument has been most explicitly advanced in the concluding chapter of *Voting*, the successor volume to *The People's Choice*. The authors here contend that the democratic system will only be viable if the majority of voters are not in fact too deeply involved in politics. Is not apathy, they suggest, a political good?

If this is so, then the terms in which democracy can be supported or attacked will be very different from those which political philosophers have up to now been used to. The champions of mass democracy may find themselves advocating it not because it maximizes popular participation in government, but because it dilutes it. Partisanship, once allowed to spread and flourish unchecked, will be seen to cause what we know as democracy to break down altogether. But we must be careful not to go too far. Before committing political philosophers to quite such a radical reappraisal of democratic theory, it will be prudent to look at the apathy argument with a distinction in mind which is not adequately applied by the authors of *Voting*. When we do, we shall see that the old democratic theories are perhaps not quite so outdated as they appeared; but we shall also see that to settle the matter we must, far from ignoring the sociologists of politics, go back to them for further evidence.

The distinction is between two possible senses of apathy. In the first sense, the apathetic voter is one who may scarcely care as between Conservative and Labour policies, or Republican and Democrat, but who would nevertheless be prepared to be active in defence of both of them against a serious extremist challenge to the system as such. In the second sense, the apathetic voter is one who is quite indifferent to the rules and forms of a democratic system, but who will vote happily for Stalin or Franco or Peron if this is the easiest thing to do. The two are not, of course, exclusive categories. Many who are indifferent as between parties under a non-totalitarian system may be also, or for just this reason, indifferent about the system itself. Equally, the most militant opponents of an attempt to subvert a non-totalitarian regime may be not the active supporters of democracy but the supporters of an alternative extremism. But we must none the less separate the two. A low level of interest, or information, or turnout at elections may mean different things. It may be interpreted, as the authors of *Voting* suggest, as indicative of the moderation, stability and even content of the electorate at large. In this case, we may call it 'good' apathy which a greater partisanship might threaten. But it may also be the sort of apathy of the Weimar electorate, many of whom had been indifferent to the existing parties until they turned out to vote for Nazism. The problem, clearly, is to tell which is which.

The sample surveys are once again our best evidence, but it is, as always, not wholly straightforward to interpret them. We know something about the characteristics of the people who are least likely to vote, least likely to be informed on current events and so on. Broadly (and as one would expect), the more prosperous a person is the more likely he is to be politically active and informed. But any conclusions drawn from this about the likelihood of support for anti-democratic movements must be cautiously drawn. We can never be sure how people would behave either under different historical circumstances or—a point which I shall come back to—under a different political system presenting them with a different range of choices. All we can do is contrast the different attitudes expressed by different social groups under the given conditions.

Two sorts of generalization have been best substantiated, though they are not always easy to distinguish. We may characterize a selected category of people either by the extent of their radicalism (how many vote for parties dedicated to changing the *status quo*) or by its degree (how many vote for parties dedicated to abolishing the system); the possibility of ambiguity arises because we may mean either or both when we say that 'miners are more radical than bank managers'. As a simple numerical example will show, they need not coincide: if the miners are 10 per cent Communist, 75 per cent Socialist and 15 per cent Conservative whereas the bank managers are 20 per cent Fascist, 30 per cent Socialist and 50 per cent Conservative, then in one sense—according to the definition just given—miners are more radical than bank managers, but in the other, bank managers are more radical than miners. If we are going to philosophize about democracy, we must be sure what sort of proposition will constitute evidence in support of our argument—a generalization about the causes of leftism, or (not the same thing) of extremism.

The second is, obviously, rather more important to those concerned about the viability of democracy. If we look at the twentieth-century history of British democracy, it is from the point of view of stability a good case for the defenders of the electorate: however much ignorance or prejudice may underlie the gentle move to the Left, it would seem to have taken place with an aggregate moderation which only Trotskyists or Empire Loyalists are (for opposite reasons) likely to deplore. What is worrying to the defenders of democracy is rather those cases where an electorate no more ignorant or prejudiced than the British produces movements genuinely subversive of the total system—movements in which, from the standpoint of the democrat, the leadership is too little apathetic but the potential following too much so. These cases can be argued to show how the 'apathetics', who may be good for a stable system on the *Voting* argument, may be the greatest threat to it under more unstable conditions. Nazism is of course the most striking and best documented example, but it is not the only one. Nor does it give a warrant for claiming that the same thing could never happen elsewhere. Any generalization about the origins and consequences of totalitarian movements depends on a greater understanding than has yet been reached about the necessary as well as the sufficient conditions for their occurrence.

There is a large literature on the topic, particularly on Nazism. But here, far more than in dealing with even the most difficult elections as such, we are doing history and not science. There is no criterion for choosing among the explanations offered, let alone for assigning the correct causal proportion for each. Once again, there is the rivalry between psychological and social explanations—were people Nazis because of defeat and inflation, or because of their toilet training, or both? And, once again, it is difficult to see how we could possibly obtain the necessary evidence for settling our choice. However, the situation is not quite so gloomy as this implies. As with the voting studies, which indeed furnish part of the evidence on this second topic, we may not know why extremists become so but we have a fairly good idea of what sort of people they are. I only want to mention one generalization which has come out of this, which is neither wholly original nor thoroughly established, but which shows the sort of evidence which a theory of democracy might use in its support. This generalization, which we met already *à propos* of fishermen and sheep-shearers, is about the effects of social isolation. It is a theme which crops up in many forms in both philosophical and empirical writings about society. It is an important part of the discussion of (in a number of its senses) alienation, and it is a worry expressed in authors as diverse as Tocqueville, Marx, William Morris, Erich Fromm and many more others than are worth enumerating. The solutions offered for the problems which it raises have ranged all the way from 'togetherness' to feudalism. For the moment, however, I only want to see how it may bear on our conclusions about political extremism.

A good deal of evidence on this specific issue has been summarized in a recent American work entitled *The Politics of Mass Society*, by William Kornhauser. Professor Kornhauser first suggests that political extremism correlates with rapidity or violence of social change (urbanization, industrialization, and so on)—a diagnosis very similar to Durkheim's in the classic essay on *Suicide*. But he also presents evidence for the sort of people most attracted to extremist movements in a given case. I give his own summary: 'Lower social strata are more responsive to mass appeals than are higher strata. However, *within all strata*, those with the fewest social ties are the most receptive to mass appeals. The first-named social category in each of the following pairs possesses the fewer social ties and is the more responsive to mass movements: (*a*) free-lance intellectuals *v.* intellectuals in corporate bodies (e.g. universities); (*b*) new business *v.* old business; (*c*) small business *v.* big business; (*d*) unskilled workers *v.* skilled workers; (*e*) mining and maritime workers *v.* workers in other kinds of industry; (*f*) poorer farmers and farm labourers *v.* wealthier farmers; (*g*) youth (especially students) *v.* adults; (*h*) politically apathetic *v.* politically involved; (*i*) unemployed *v.* employed.'[1]

These conclusions are perhaps not surprising. The extremism of, for instance, students and unemployed workers will not be new to the historian of nineteenth-century Europe, where this explosive combination more than once brought governments to their knees. But the interest of Kornhauser's findings is how general they are. Some, needless to say, are less well substantiated than others. But assuming without argument that they are more or less correct, is there not a clear implication for political theory? Professor Kornhauser's recommendation is the same as Tocqueville's: strengthen the social ties. If, accordingly, this is what is important for democracy to work, the basic prescriptions of democratic theory should perhaps be made less directly political than hitherto. On this argument (which assumes, of course, that a Sorelian putsch, whether from Left or Right, is what we wish to avoid), it should be the aim of the democratic theorist to encourage people into as many *non*-political associations as possible.

But even supposing that this argument can be thoroughly substantiated (and it can, of course, be much less crudely put than I have done here), there are questions left unanswered. Let us return to the British case, and to the assumption that (without implying further comparisons) the recent history of British democracy can be favourably contrasted with that of Germany or France. Even if all the generalizations about social isolation are true, how can it be shown that they are more than very marginally relevant as compared to much broader institutional factors? And until this can be proved, are we entitled to pronounce that our theories of democracy must be reshaped to take account of these generalizations? The most consistent correlations from the sample surveys may be wholly unimportant until we can give the answer which neither Marx, nor Halévy nor anybody else has been able to give to the one big historical question: why no revolution in England?

This immense and provocative subject is far beyond the scope of these essays. But it leads me to the last sort of generalization by a political scientist which I want to look at for its relevance to political theory. One of the arguments put forward to explain the stability of British politics derives not from either the social or the psychological attributes of the British elector but the rules governing the system itself. The two-party system is sometimes pointed to by its admirers as a splendid and uniquely British invention by which feeble coalitions, splintered parties, extremist electorates and all the other vices of continental politics have been mercifully and wisely strangled at birth. This formulation is a little flippant. But there is a perfectly serious case for saying that the electoral system of any given country plays a major or even fundamental role in moulding the political behaviour of its citizens. The most cogent generalization on this topic is Professor Duverger's (whose book on *Political Parties* I have already referred to). The generalization, and the ambitious claim which Professor Duverger makes for it, can be found on p. 217 of this same work. 'The influence of...national factors', says Duverger, 'is certainly very considerable; but we must not in their favour underestimate the importance of one general factor of a technical kind, the electoral system. Its effect can be expressed in the following formula: *the simple-majority single-ballot system favours the two-party system*. Of all the hypotheses that have been defined in this book, this approaches the most nearly perhaps to a true sociological law. An almost complete correlation is observable between the simple-majority single-ballot system and the two-party system: dualist countries use the simple-majority vote and simple-majority vote countries are dualist. The exceptions are very rare and can generally be explained as the result of special conditions.'

This is a large claim. Moreover, if it is true, it will have just as clear an implication for the political theorist as those findings we have earlier been looking at. If the electoral system is the principal determinant of the party system and can serve to inhibit altogether the rise of smaller and more extremist parties, then we find ourselves being led back to that tradition of political theory whereby it is the conscious moulding of institutions by legislators about which prescriptive suggestions should be made. Unfortunately, however, the Duverger doctrine, as it is sometimes called,[1] has been subjected to some damaging criticism. In the first place, Duverger's presentation of his doctrine has been shown not to be altogether consistent; secondly, the evidence is in fact less easy to square with it than Duverger suggests; thirdly, it is doubtful if Duverger's psychological assumptions are entirely plausible.

I shall not reproduce these criticisms in detail. There can be little doubt that Duverger's case is less strong than he makes it, for even the British case—which to Duverger is a long-run reversion to bi-partism—can be interpreted to tell against the doctrine rather than in favour of it. The fact that Labour could take over from the Liberals at all is strong evidence against Duverger's claim that supporters of third parties feel that they will be throwing away their votes. Moreover, the consistent Irish representation at Westminster throughout the late nineteenth century and earlier twentieth is surely best described as three established parties operating in a simple-majority, single-ballot system.

The most important factor is the constituency effect, which Duverger does not mention. Any third party can obtain consistent representation under the British system which draws on a type of support concentrated in particular constituencies. This was true of the Irish Nationalists and in many important instances of the Labour Party. It is only true to a small extent of the Liberals (at any rate at the time of writing). Of course, proportional representation would on any plausible set of assumptions have greatly benefited the Liberals in Britain since 1922. But this is much less than what Duverger is saying.

However, it is equally hard to argue that there is nothing whatever in the Duverger doctrine; and this is particularly the case when considering the emergence of the sort of extremist parties which I have principally been talking about. It may be, as Duverger's critics argue, that there are no grounds for supposing that to introduce proportional representation where it does not exist will actually increase the number of parties—it happened in Holland, for instance, but not in Belgium, where it only rescued a declining Liberal party. But if proportional representation is strictly applied—if, that is, there is no arbitrary quotient system designed to abort all parties securing less than a fixed minimum of support—there would appear to be a definite multiplicative effect. Similarly, there seems to be a clearly discernible effect on the pattern of electoral support produced by the double ballot. Here, the best-known case is France. Under the Third Republic, in 1932, the Communists refused to combine with other parties for the second ballot and received only 8 per cent of the first ballot vote. In 1936, when they joined the Popular Front, their share of the first ballot vote was doubled and their representation rose from 11 seats to 72. Under the Fourth

Republic, with proportional representation, 150 Communists held seats in the final parliament. Under the Fifth Republic, which returned to the double-ballot, single-constituency system, the number of Communists went down almost to single figures. I am not suggesting—and nor, I am sure, would Professor Duverger—that these fluctuations were the sole result of the changes in the electoral system. But there is surely a good case for saying that they are at least in part a result of it.

If it is possible firmly to establish conclusions of this kind, then there would seem to be a number of recommendations which the constitutional theorists can make for the provision and appraisal of checks against extremism. If specific legislation can markedly further the two-party system, and if (as other writers than Duverger have argued) there is always a tendency in a two-party system for the two parties to assimilate to each other,[1] then the theorist of democracy has once more to frame his recommendations within a definite context of established facts about its workings. I do not mean that generalizations such as Duverger's could ever reduce all constitutional questions about electoral reform to administrative technicalities directed to an agreed end. There is an area of disagreement between the supporters and opponents of proportional representation which reflects a genuine dilemma for the political theorist. There is an obvious sense in which proportional representation is more 'fair'; but there is an equally genuine case to be made for the present constituency system and for the need to encourage stronger government even at the expense of more accurate representation of opinion. Many of the questions are, of course, technical; and in addition, the debate has often been argued more with a view to electoral advantage than to theoretical principle. But the issue of principle is there. What I am suggesting is only that evidence such as Duverger's is a necessary ingredient of any defence of a prescriptive position on these topics.

It may still be doubtful whether any wholly unequivocal implications for the political theorist have emerged out of all the researches of political sociologists since elections have begun to be systematically studied. Indeed, the conclusion which follows from what I have been talking about is perhaps rather to diminish the 'scientific' status of political science than to claim for it any capacity to solve the problems of political theory. The more of such evidence that is produced, the more difficult it is to feel sure how far similar cases are really comparable. As I argued in chapter 1, one of the two ineluctable limitations on social science is the uniqueness of every historical sequence, and any generalization about who votes for whom (let alone why) must be suspect if only on this ground. But despite this, there is ample evidence that it would be a mistake to be frightened off any attempt to generalize at all. These generalizations embody the empirical evidence which the political theorist must take account of in framing his recommendations; and however provisional these generalizations may be, the moral to be drawn is surely that the empirical and philosophical study of politics have more to gain from a maximum contact with each other than many of their practitioners—whether American sociologists or Oxford philosophers—have been apt to suppose.

CHAPTER VI

METHODS, MODELS AND THEORIES

Even if it is a mistake to look for general theories of society, and even if all theories in the social sciences are bound to be subject to limitations from which the natural sciences are exempt, it is still worth asking how far any particular social science may have progressed in the direction of a full-fledged theory. In political science, there is in fact one and only one serious candidate for such a theory—using theory in its non-prescriptive sense—apart from Marxism. Not even its strongest partisans would yet argue that it has produced a set of propositions about political behaviour comparable in scope or force to those of Marxism. But they would, despite this concession, claim that an alternative set of general propositions can be formulated which provide a better explanation of the known facts of political behaviour than Marxism has done. This alternative approach to Marxism is the functionalist approach, which I have already referred to. I am only really concerned with its application to specifically political systems of institutions and behaviour. But it shares with Marxism the important characteristic of setting out to provide an explanation of all social processes; and before, therefore, considering its relevance to the theorist (in either the prescriptive or the non-prescriptive sense) of politics, we shall have to make some brief assessment of this general claim. In doing so, moreover, we shall find that functionalism, like even the most scientific Marxism, turns out in several ways to look more like a philosophy of politics than the general sociological theory which its supporters claim it to be.

Functionalism, as I remarked in chapter 1, came into the social sciences from biology; and in some ways this is less of a novelty than it might seem, because organic analogies and modes of reasoning about the body politic and its members are of very ancient origin. But the main impact of what is now meant by functionalism on the social sciences may be fairly dated from 1922, when there appeared the two classics of functionalism, Malinowski's *Argonauts of the Western Pacific* and Radcliffe-Brown's *Andaman Islanders*. There are a number of differences between Malinowski and Radcliffe-Brown, as between many other subsequent functionalists, so that to lump them together involves something of an oversimplification. Both, however, exemplify what is common to the functionalist approach in all its forms, which is to ask in studying a given social or political system not how a pattern of behaviour may have originated so much as what part it plays in maintaining the system as a whole. This represented at the time a salutary shift of emphasis. It was a useful departure from the sort of conjectural evolutionary history which had been the previous anthropological fashion, and it was a good antidote against any implicit disdain for the habits of undeveloped or 'primitive' peoples. Obviously, it is more sensible when studying a polygamous society to look for the way in which polygamy helps to keep the society going than to treat it as a retrograde stage in the 'normal' evolution towards Christian monogamy. But functionalism, however useful as a shift of emphasis, has as a theory of social processes been subjected to some damaging logical criticisms.

Two often-quoted passages from Malinowski and Radcliffe-Brown may be cited as illustrations of classic—or, one should perhaps say, old-fashioned—functionalism. First, Malinowski: 'In every type of civilisation, every custom, material object, idea and belief fulfils some vital function, has some task to accomplish, represents an indispensable part within a working whole.'[1] This assertion, though it carries the useful implication that nothing in any society should be taken for granted, is nevertheless either quite obviously false or else true only by definition. As Radcliffe-Brown himself points out in one essay, it is unlikely that the taboo against spilling salt in our own society has any social function;[2] and if Malinowski means that everything accomplishes some task simply by virtue of existing as it is and not otherwise, then this is merely a trivial assertion to the effect that everything in a society must be just as it is for the total society to be just as it is.

Radcliffe-Brown's own formulation, however, is not very much less open to objection. He does not maintain that every teaspoon or neurosis in a given civilization is essential to it. But he claims that 'the function of any recurrent activity, such as the punishment of a crime or a funeral ceremony, is the part it plays in the social life as a whole and therefore the contribution it makes to the maintenance of the structural continuity'.[3] This is, perhaps, at first sight more plausible (or less trivial); but there is, as Radcliffe-Brown's critics have rightly detected,[4] a crucial flaw in the 'therefore'. Radcliffe-Brown's assertion is just as much as Malinowski's either an obvious falsehood or else an unhelpful tautology. To say that it follows from the fact that a recurrent activity plays a part in the social life as a whole that it therefore helps to maintain the structural continuity, is only true if any recurrent activity is by definition part of the continuity to which it must contribute by its mere occurrence. It should be made clear that these two statements are of a much less subtle version of functionalism than any of its advocates would nowadays put forward. But the difficulties which the two statements clearly involve persist even in more sophisticated versions of functionalism, and are enough to prevent functionalism from ever becoming an explanatory theory of social processes.

The central difficulty is this: it is mistaken to suppose that a behaviour-pattern which is shown to have an important effect on the total social structure has thereby been explained. As Durkheim pointed out a good many years before Malinowski, to show how something is useful is not to explain how it originated or why it is what it is.[1] It may do so in the case where conscious purposes are at work, for here (and here only) an occurrence or a pattern of behaviour may be explained by reference to its results. But to explain something as a result of the intentions of given persons does not necessarily require the notion of functionalism. Biologists may, on occasion, speak in such phrases as plants having roots 'in order to' extract nourishment from the soil. But the phrase is not intended to imply a conscious purpose, but simply observed results (unless, of course, it is God's purpose which is in the speaker's mind). Functionalist terms may also be used (as is done by Malinowski) for determinism by needs, as in the statement that getting food is a functional prerequisite for the continuing existence of any human society. But this is very obviously trivial; and though it may become interesting when a pattern of behaviour is seen as deriving from the need to acquire food or to limit its consumption, this once again does not have to be deduced from a functionalist theory. That an institution may survive its original purpose because it comes to satisfy some other need is a phenomenon familiar to any historian. But it is a phenomenon which can be as well or better explained in historical terms than teleological ones. Similarly, it may be interesting to suggest that because of a universal need among mankind for some form of organized religion the messianic appeal of Marxism may be better understood. But this does not enable us to deduce the actual spread of Marxism from a functionalist theory whereby the messianic urges of mankind must somehow or other be fulfilled.

A number of other accusations have been levelled against functionalism, notably that it is incapable of accounting for historical change. But this is secondary to the main issue, quite apart from the fact that self-styled functionalists have often claimed to explain specific historical changes. The prior question is whether functionalism can provide an explanatory theory at all, and on this the central point is a very simple one: any meaningful statement in terms of 'function' can without loss of meaning be translated into an 'if...then' statement of cause and effect. It can be shown that in the case of all self-regulating systems where functionalist language is most often and appropriately used, such statements can be effectively formalized.[1] This does not mean, however, that the use of functionalist terminology, even where most appropriate, subsumes the causal proposition concerned under a general explanatory theory. It may help the investigator in his search for one; but this is hardly the same thing.

It has, in fact, been argued that this help to the investigator should be seen as the sole usefulness of functionalist language: it directs him to particular statements of cause and effect about 'self-regulation' or 'adaptation' or 'universal prerequisites' which he might otherwise be less likely to discern.[2] It has also been suggested that functionalist analysis is in fact synonymous with sociological analysis in general, and that we should therefore be well advised to stop talking about 'functionalism' altogether.[1] However, the proponents of functionalism still champion it as a distinctive approach which can lead to, although it may not yet constitute, an explanatory theory of some or even all social processes. Before, therefore, considering this claim as it applies in particular to politics, it is worth asking whether there are any particular kinds of statement of sociological cause and effect for which functionalist terminology may be both heuristically useful and logically defensible. The view which I want to suggest is that there are two and only two types of such statements.

The first type is where the analogy from biology is in fact appropriate—that is to say, where it is possible to specify the extreme permissible limits of certain variables such that where these limits are exceeded the system breaks down. Perhaps the most familiar example is the temperature of the human body and the homeostatic mechanisms which exist 'for the purpose of'—that is, with the effect of— maintaining it within the acceptable limits. The difficulty when this notion is applied to social, economic or political systems rather than to biological ones is that it becomes much more difficult to define in advance the acceptable limits; but a functionalist analysis can still be made logically unexceptionable. The language and procedures of cybernetics are likely to be useful for this purpose. When a system has been defined as a set of variables, then a subset of the possible values of these variables can be designated as constituting the range of acceptable states. In the case of an economic system, the acceptable states might be any subset of possibilities which excluded those involved in the definition of 'slump'. In the case of a political system, they might be any subset which excluded those involved in the definition of 'anarchy' or 'civil war'. But however they are

Methods, Models and Theories

defined (and their good or bad definition is a separate, though difficult, issue) it becomes possible to ask what aspects of the system's state or behaviour may be regarded as 'functional'. This is the same, in other words, as asking what serves to keep the essential variables of the system within their predefined acceptable limits. This still does not amount to an explanation, let alone a theory, of the behaviour involved. But it makes it possible to isolate those particular relations or suggested relations of cause and effect which, if the functionalist approach has the merits which are claimed for it, are most likely to lead the investigator to such an explanation on the lines of 'functional interdependence', 'reciprocal causality', 'dynamic equilibrium' and so on.

The second type of statement where functionalist terminology may be useful and where it may be employed without logical disaster is a statement which is, in fact, about purposes. I do not mean by this only individual intentions, as in such cases as 'Hitler wanted the war', but cases where it is possible to speak unambiguously about the 'goals' of a system as such. This is perfectly possible, but only provided that we can avoid the two chief dangers which occur in practice. Both of these arise from the fact that the concept of 'goal' presupposes the notion of 'purpose'. The first is the difficulty to which, as I have mentioned, any full-scale functional theory is liable, namely that purposes cannot properly be spoken of when only observed results are meant. The second is that even where purposes are not being confused with results, it must be possible to specify the particular persons whose specific purposes are meant. The first of these points is obvious enough: when, for instance, a well-known anthropological textbook speaks of distinguishing an 'ulterior' purpose construed by the observer from the 'proximate' purpose of the actors whom he observes,[1] it would clearly be less misleading to speak of results or, perhaps, utility than of 'ulterior purposes'; similarly, Lévi-Strauss has been quite rightly criticized for making human intelligence his efficient cause when he argues that tribesmen adopt their rules governing exchanges of women between kin-groups literally 'in order to' preserve and increase the solidarity of their societies by means of such exchanges.[2] The second difficulty, however, may be harder to deal with, and deserves separate comment.

We are certainly not required to limit the notion of purpose to single, conscious intentions implemented by individual persons. It is, for instance, perfectly legitimate to speak of the explanatory validity of a learning model, or of a 'purposeful' machine such as a torpedo with a target-seeking mechanism. But an adequate explanation of observed behaviour in terms of goals must involve not only a description of the mechanism by which a goal is pursued but also an ascertained purpose on the part of a designated person or set of persons. This applies directly in the case of any social system. We must be able to specify the values of the 'state coordinates' of the system which constitute the purpose of designated members (present or past) of that system. If we cannot, then the concept of 'goal-attainment' can have no value either for the explanation of particular findings or for the formulation of some more general theory. Moreover, we must know in advance what sort of evidence would entitle us to reject an assertion of the form 'the goal of system S is X', for only with this can we assign an unambiguous meaning to assertions of the form 'A is functional for S' in this second sense.

Sometimes this is straightforward enough. For example, the main organizational objectives of bureaucratic agencies can in general be clearly defined,[1] or it can be legitimately asserted that 'the goal of any specific industry is to add value to its typical products'.[2] But when we try to consider a total society, as opposed to a definable political, economic or familial system (or set of variables), it becomes immediately clear that there are unlikely to be any such readily definable objectives. Do we mean by the goals of a total society the purposes of its effective rulers, or the wishes of the majority of its members, or the principles written into its constitution by its founders? Professor Talcott Parsons, whose contention it is that goal-attainment is a 'functional prerequisite' of all social systems, never seems to consider this problem. One of many historical examples would be France between the revolution of 1848 and the *coup d'état* of Louis Napoleon in 1851. It is difficult to see by what criteria it could be established what the 'societal goals' of France as such were during this period, or, indeed, whether France had any 'societal goals' at all. But the only alternative to this, on the basis of Parsons's assertion, is to say that during this period France was not a social system at all for precisely this reason. In this case, however, it becomes clear that the claim that goal-attainment is a functional prerequisite for all social systems is neither a theory nor even an empirical generalization but a tautology.

We can, however, without tumbling into such pitfalls as these, make functionalist statements about causes and effects related either to the predefined acceptable states of the system concerned or to the designated purposes of persons whom it is plausible in some sense to identify with the system. In both cases, a sense can be given to the adaptation or adjustment of the system which the observed patterns of behaviour are presumed by functionalists to help to bring about. In neither case, moreover, need such notions presuppose a value-judgement in the way that many of the opponents of functionalism have been apt to argue and even some of its champions to concede. Nadel, for example, goes so far as to allow that 'If we do not employ the function concept we cannot speak of adjustment; yet if we employ it, we must be prepared to judge by ultimate values'.[1] This, as I hope the foregoing discussion has made clear, need not be so, provided that we are careful about defining our terms. Two senses can be given to 'functional', 'adjustment' and similar terms where no question of 'ultimate values' is involved. It is a question only of concern with particular types of statement of cause and effect, or, more precisely, with the question whether a given pattern of behaviour tends to produce a result tending to cause the system to change in a predefined direction. Whether this is useful or not will be a further question.

It can be strongly argued that the functionalist approach has in fact proved useful, if only in directing the observer's attention to the possibilities of a particular type of cause and effect which may help to explain what puzzles him. A good example from political behaviour may be taken from the work of Professor Merton, whose essay on 'Manifest and Latent Functions' remains one of the clearest and most useful discussions by a sympathetic critic. Merton shows how the phenomenon of American boss-politics may be readily understood by seeing it as satisfying needs generated by the American social structure which are not otherwise met. In Merton's own words, 'The functional deficiencies of the official structure generate an alternative (unofficial) structure to fulfil existing needs somewhat more effectively. Whatever its specific historical origins, the machine persists as an apparatus for satisfying otherwise unfulfilled needs of diverse groups in the population.'[2] Machine-politics arise, on Merton's analysis, because there are large sub-groups within the American population for whose needs the existing legal and political institutions are inadequate. On top of this, the American ethic of competitive success imposes on all members of American society a compulsion towards a type of goal which minority ethnic groups are in practice denied many of the means to achieve. The result is Tammany Hall. That this line of argument, which I have briefly summarized, serves to account for much of the pattern of big-city politics in the United States would, as far as I know, be generally agreed by all those who have studied it. Accordingly, Merton's discussion may be claimed as a good example of how the functionalist presupposition of needs being consciously or unconsciously met helps us to understand a particular structure of institutions and behaviour. But it remains necessary to stress that a complete explanation cannot be given except in historical terms. It is not a case of deducing American politics from a general law about the fulfilment of political needs, but a case of the sort of general notion of psychological cause and effect which all historical explanations must at some point rest on. Merton's analysis is social and political history, not codified science. To see the inadequacy of an attempt to interpret findings about political behaviour in terms of a would-be general functionalist theory it is worth turning to Parsons's discussion of the findings of the American voting studies.

In an essay entitled '*Voting* and the Equilibrium of the American Political System', Parsons takes the findings of the second of the Lazarsfeld studies and argues that they support his general functionalist-type theory. But how the findings either confirm his general theory or are explained by it is very far from clear. At one point Parsons states only that they fit 'with a more general conceptual scheme', but a few lines later he is claiming that they fit closely with deductions from 'highly general theory'. On the other hand, a footnote allows that this is 'very different from deducing the *specific* findings of the empirical research. Of course this has not been done.'[1] It is difficult, in all this, to make out just what Parsons is claiming for his 'theory'. There is the confusion between a theory and a conceptual scheme, or between classification and analysis, which I mentioned in chapter 1 and which Parsons's critics have detected throughout his work. But in any case, even if we should be prepared to concede that Parsons is putting forward what can in some sense be properly designated a theory, it is not a theory amenable to adequate validation or falsification. At one point, Parsons does seem to be aware of this, for he assigns to his schema only a heuristic value, and says that 'By applying the model to the general structure it was possible to identify four main areas in which to look for mechanisms relevant to these functional requirements'.[2] But if this is what Parsons is really saying, it only defers the problems of explanation one step further. Even the heuristic value of the conceptual scheme is not justified until a testable, non-tautologous assertion of 'if...then' form has been put forward which (as in Merton's case) can explain, at least in part, the behaviour under discussion. The findings of *Voting* may well constitute evidence for such an assertion as 'American politics follow a relatively stable pattern', and this is an assertion which Parsons might wish to maintain to be true. But no redescription of the findings in terms of 'integration' or 'pattern-maintenance' can properly answer the question 'why?'.

This brings us to the basic issue. The presupposition that social systems, of whatever kind, have a built-in tendency to equilibrium is as undemonstrable, and therefore as

Methods, Models and Theories

incapable of providing satisfactory explanations, as the assumptions underlying Marxism. Functionalism, as a theory, is not a set of causal laws but an interpretation which places a prior emphasis and value on the normative elements of social systems, just as Marxism places a prior emphasis and value on the essential conflicts which it points to in such systems. The point has been simply made against Parsons by David Lockwood in a discussion of Parsons's book *The Social System*: 'Why', asks Lockwood, 'has Parsons given conceptual priority to the normative structuring of action?'[1] And the answer, of course, is that Parsons wishes to make an assumption which precedes and cannot be deduced from the analysis of the social relations which he describes. Parsons cannot prove that the factors in society which make for agreement and harmony are fundamentally more important than those making for disagreement and conflict. Just as we saw in the case of Marx, such assumptions can never be proved, but only, like all philosophical standpoints, well or badly defended. It is not a case of rival systems of laws, like Ptolemaic astronomy versus Copernican, but of rival interpretations of human actions.

Functionalism can, indeed, be interpreted as a conscious alternative to Marxism. Some of its critics have even wanted to interpret it as a political ideology conditioned by the structure of American capitalism. But leaving aside the separate issue of its historical origins, it is interesting to notice just how far functionalism provides a sort of mirror-image of Marxism. In both cases, the crux of interpretation rests on assumptions which cannot be strictly proved from the evidence of historical fact; but each theory claims to offer a better interpretation of all the known facts than can the other. 'Look,' says the Marxist, 'don't you see that there is a fundamental conflict between the classes? This is the basic fact of politics, resulting from the iron laws of economic determinism.' 'Look,' says the functionalist, 'don't you see that there is a fundamental harmony in the role-structure of society? This is the basic fact of politics, resulting from the way in which patterns of behaviour emerge in response to the needs felt by all human societies.' Neither claim is wholly absurd, but nor is it wholly demonstrable. Moreover, both sides claim to be able to incorporate precisely the evidence most relied upon by the other. 'Apparent identity of interest', says the Marxist, 'is merely a distortion in the ideological superstructure produced by the economic base.' 'Conflict', says the functionalist, 'is really functional, for by releasing or resolving tensions it enables a society better to adjust.' There is no evidence which both sides could agree on as constituting a definitive test of their rival views. If they are to persuade each other, they must persuade each other on philosophical grounds to adopt an alternative view of the world.

The fact remains, however, that some form of functionalism is the only current alternative to Marxism as the basis for some kind of general theory in political science. We have already seen, in chapter II, the danger involved in attempting a functionalist definition of the State; and this chapter has suggested grounds for scepticism about the capacity of functionalism to provide full explanations of political or other social behaviour. But its usefulness must be assessed by the value of the explanatory propositions to which it guides the investigator of a particular problem. It may, if nothing else, provide a framework for the comparative discussion of different political systems, for which the vocabulary of traditional political theory is no longer adequate. It may direct attention to causes and effects which would otherwise pass unnoticed. It may even help in clarifying some of the problems of traditional political theory, such as the 'collective purpose' or 'general will' of society as expounded by some of the idealist philosophers.[1] It is only as a would-be general theory that it becomes more likely to be misleading than helpful, and to by-pass the search for the rigorous and testable statements of cause and effect out of which a political science is to be constructed. The fact is that the empirical methods, rather than the deductive theories, of political science have since Marx and Weber been more productive of such statements. These methods have not, perhaps, produced quite so close an approximation to natural science as some of their practitioners have claimed. But there can be little doubt that they have greatly advanced the search for better explanations of political behaviour, and a brief discussion of their scientific status is in order at this point.

I do not mean to try to summarize, or even to mention, all the methods which are available to the sociologist of politics. Different methods, whether anthropological, historical or statistical, are appropriate to different problems and they must be judged, like functionalist or other theories, by the value of the explanatory propositions to which they lead. But the more recent of them are on the whole the more statistical and those for which the most 'scientific' claims are apt to be made. With their help, questions of an unaccustomed precision can be answered which may lead to the far more accurate detection of correlations between social phenomena than it had previously been possible to envisage. The question, therefore, is whether they can make possible the sort of statements of correlation which have, at their most successful, yielded the laws of natural science. The danger here is not so much the simple danger of mistaking correlation for causation, for this is no less possible in the natural sciences. The danger is rather that of supposing that all the precautions of natural sciences can be so reproduced that we may ultimately be led to laws of political behaviour strictly analogous to the laws which govern the behaviour of such natural phenomena as gases or electric currents.

The general point can perhaps be best illustrated by reference to the techniques of the sample survey. With the remarkable development of sampling techniques I am not concerned so much as with the way in which survey data can be analysed so as to elucidate a presumed causal relation. The method used for this, and developed most notably by Professor Lazarsfeld, is that of holding one factor constant in order to test the effect of others. Suppose, for example, that a sample survey shows a correlation between religion and party affiliation: the great majority of Protestants are Republican, and the great majority of Catholics are Democrat. If, before the days of survey analysis, someone were to object to such a generalization on the grounds that it is wealth or poverty which determines voting, and it is only a coincidence that wealth and poverty also correlate with being Protestant or Catholic, there would have been no accurate way of testing this counter-assertion. But with a sample survey this is in fact perfectly feasible. We can break the sample down further into rich and poor, and see whether within the rich and poor (taken as separate categories) the correlation between religion and party affiliation still holds good. More precisely still, we can see just to what extent and under what conditions this kind of correlation holds good, and we can test how much of the variation in the behaviour which we observe can be accounted for by different causal factors.

In Lazarsfeld's terminology, there are three basic operations of this kind which can be performed on survey data: explanation, interpretation and specification. These are used in a special sense, but examples make them readily clear. 'Explanation' is when a spurious correlation is explained away by the introduction of a third factor into the analysis. An excellent example of Lazarsfeld's is the proposition (which is true) that the more fire engines come to a fire, the more damage is done. This correlation is only puzzling until we remember that the reason why more fire engines come to a fire in the first place is that the fire is a big one, and the true causal relation is between the size of the fire and the amount of damage which it does. 'Interpretation' is when there is an 'intervening variable' between the two phenomena which are correlated with each other, and we wish to say not that X causes Y but that X causes something which in its turn causes Y. Lazarsfeld gives as an example the finding that during the Second World War married women working in factories had a higher rate of absenteeism than unmarried women. The clue to this correlation is not, of course, that married women were lazier or less patriotic but that because of being married they had other responsibilities or difficulties which caused them to have a higher rate of absenteeism. 'Specification', finally, is when the correlation between two variables is partly, but not wholly, dependent on a third factor. For example, an economic depression has a bad effect on the morale of all families, but a worse effect on authoritarian families than other types. In all three types of analysis, a causal relationship is being elucidated; and since it is in principle possible to sift out spurious correlations, it should be possible to establish causal relations as rigorously as in a controlled experiment. It is worth quoting Kendall and Lazarsfeld directly: 'The notion of explanation provides an analytic basis for defining clearly a causal relationship between two variables. If the partial relationships never disappear, even when every conceivable test factor is introduced, then the original relationship is a causal one. This definition reproduces in statistical form the situation existing in all true controlled experiments.'[1]

No one can quarrel with this claim in principle. But the danger is that of supposing that the analogue to a controlled experiment can ever be quite as close as is implied. Not only is it impossible in practice to introduce every conceivable test factor, but even where experimental controls are feasible, as in laboratory psychology, there remain the two same crucial differences between the subject-matter of natural and of social science. It is not that we need to reject on philosophical grounds the deterministic assumptions which underlie the experimental method (though some opponents of social science would wish to do so). The difficulty is that even in an experimental situation, the uniqueness of historical sequences and the meaningfulness of human action make it illegitimate to draw an exact parallel between conclusions experimentally established in natural and in social science. It is impossible to introduce every conceivable test factor because such factors may be by their nature irreplicable, and without replicability the experimental method breaks down. Moreover (and related to this), the experimenter is faced with the possibility that the conditions of the experiment may themselves so act on the persons whose conscious behaviour he is studying that they constitute an independent variable which cannot be adequately controlled. In this connection, a parallel is sometimes drawn between the difficulties confronting the social experimenter and Heisenberg's famous uncertainty prin-

Methods, Models and Theories 127

ciple in physics, according to which the physical measurement of atomic objects can only (due to the exchange of energy involved) yield knowledge of a state which is destroyed by the process of measurement and cannot therefore be known. But though the parallel is in a sense valid, it obscures the fundamental difference between the situation of the natural and the social scientist. Heisenberg's problem has indeed occasioned some metaphysical debate among philosophers of science. But the 'path' of a particle is an object of inquiry different in kind from the 'attitude' of a human subject. There may be reasons why neither can be, as it were, pinned down as it is; but the meaningful actions, as opposed to events, with which the social experimenter deals are in a further sense immune to reductive causal analysis.

Some of the difficulties to which this gives rise can, perhaps, be labelled technical. Even Popper's argument, that future knowledge constitutes an independent variable which the investigator can never allow for in formulating social predictions, may be put forward (as it is by Popper) from a standpoint of the unity of scientific method. But what remains is still the role which interpretation has to play in the social but not (or not in the same sense) in the natural sciences. In the social sciences, the use or interest of any technique of statistical correlation depends upon some intuitive notions about cause and effect which cannot be justified by residual correlation or confirmed prediction alone. In the case of the techniques of survey analysis which I discussed above, it can be formally demonstrated that 'the decision that a partial correlation is or is not spurious (does not or does indicate a causal ordering) can in general only be reached if *a priori* assumptions are made that certain *other* causal relations do *not* hold among the variables'.[1]

There is no great problem in avoiding such assertions as that the age of a person does not depend upon his political attitudes, rather than vice versa. But in attempting a full causal analysis of the political behaviour of a person or a class of persons the limitations of residual correlation become much more quickly apparent. Any proffered explanation will be bound to retain some irreducibly intuitive element, some assumptions about human motives and intentions which even the best approximation to experimental controls could not make it possible to do away with.

The misapplication of methods modelled on the natural sciences can perhaps best be illustrated from one recent dispute among methodologists of social science. This is the debate about the use of significance tests which is chiefly associated with the name of Professor Hanan Selvin of the University of California.[1] Tests of statistical significance, of which the chi-square test is the most notorious, constitute an elegant and powerful arithmetical technique for answering the question how likely it is that an observed correlation may be due to chance. If, for instance, one out of five inoculated patients contracts a given disease at the same time as three out of twelve who were not inoculated, it is possible to calculate the chance that such a correlation might have occurred if inoculation had in fact no effect whatsoever on the likelihood of any one patient catching the disease. If the correlation is not significant (in the statistical sense), then the investigator has no grounds for claiming that inoculation had a beneficial effect; if, on the other hand, there is only one chance in a hundred that such a correlation could have occurred by accident, then the hypothesis that underlay the administration of inoculation would seem to be justified. The misuse of such techniques arises, however, when they are applied (as they have been) to sample survey data, and when the fact that a correlation can be shown to be statistically significant is used as vindication of a claim that a hypothesized causal relation has been confirmed. I shall not review the fairly extensive dispute which there has been on this topic, but simply mention two points made by Selvin which would appear to demonstrate beyond dispute that the application of such tests to survey data is the indulgence of unjustifiable scientism.

In the first place, no survey fulfils the necessary conditions of a controlled experiment. It may be true that in theory these conditions could be reproduced, as it were, in retrospect, provided that information had been collected on every conceivably relevant factor. But this condition will never be realized, quite apart from the nature of the actions (as opposed to events) which are being studied. Any survey contains more possible sources of variation than can be controlled, including the technical limitations involved in carrying surveys out in practice. As long as this is so, there is no warrant for concluding that a test of significance is in fact answering the question for which it is designed. To ask whether it is possible that the given correlation is due to chance and not to the causal processes supposed by the investigator makes sense only when there is a guarantee that it cannot be due to some third factor altogether. This can be safely assumed in the case of our inoculation example, once the assignment of patients to the two groups has been made random. It can then be assumed that all the other sources of variation are randomized out, so that the experimenter is left with the choice of explanations limited to the two sole factors of chance and of inoculation. But even here, the result of a chi-square test has to be cautiously interpreted, given the possibility of bias. In a sample survey, where not even an approximation to controlled experiment is actually feasible, the test has hardly any meaning at all.

Furthermore, the question of interpretation once again shows the danger of scientism. This can be best illustrated by the example from Chapter IV. Suppose that an investigator finds two equally significant correlations between voting Labour and believing in Socialism and voting Labour and having red hair. It is obvious that it would be as absurd to ask for a significance test of the first as to claim that such a test demonstrated a causal relationship in the second. When confronted with a correlation which seems to need no further explanation for the purpose concerned, a significance test is unnecessary; when the correlation obviously needs further explanation, a significance test is irrelevant. In the second case, the results must be further broken down in terms of what could be supposed to be causal factors, and the decision to stop the analysis at a given point has to be made on interpretative, not on statistical grounds. Correlation, in fact, is no proof of causation in a sense further to that in which the maxim also applies in the natural sciences. Even in a situation where it could be claimed that a social investigator had allowed for every conceivable factor, there are correlations which, however significant, he would on intuitive grounds be bound to reject. No amount of significance testing makes convincing the assertion that a man's politics are determined by the colour of his hair. It might be that colour of hair is correlated with some other genetic factor which relates to political attitudes, or that in a given country red-headed men are members of an ethnic minority whose interests differ from those of the blond or black-haired majority. But in such a case, it is not red-headedness as such which is the determinant. Given a choice of significant correlations, the causal factor will be chosen on

Methods, Models and Theories

intuitive grounds even if an experimental study design has been as closely followed as possible.

The moral, clearly, is that any statistical techniques must be the servants, not the masters, of interpretation. It may be, for instance, that it is occasionally useful to know whether the correlation which an investigator wishes on interpretative grounds to put forward as causal might not be statistically explicable in terms of chance simply as far as the actual distribution of cases is concerned. It might then be wise to be more cautious about the proffered conclusion than if the figures were clearly not explicable by random distribution. But this is a very different use of statistical reasoning from the interminable chi-squares of the sociological journals, where the need to turn the obvious into the scientific seems sometimes the only justification for a spurious apparatus of exactitude.

Techniques of correlation are an extraordinarily useful tool in the organization of data, but they are never in themselves a means to their explanation. Factor analysis—the most sophisticated of the correlational techniques normally employed by sociologists of politics—provides only a further example. The technique, whose application in the social sciences has been largely in the field of psychometric studies, provides for the reduction of observed variations into the components which may serve (statistically) to account for the greater part of them. Attitudes to a political party might, for instance, be shown to derive largely from two or three basic viewpoints, which could account for most of the variance found in responses to a questionnaire designed to elicit all possible facets of popular attitudes to that party.[1] But this once again only enables the question 'why?' to be more precisely and economically formulated. This may be of great use to the investigator, if only in enabling him to dispose of a number of possible interpretations. But it will not solve for him the problem of choosing the right one. All this is perhaps very obvious; but it is sufficiently neglected both by the partisans and the opponents of social science to be worth repeating. It is a mistake to suppose that the fetishists of quantitative techniques will ever be able to turn the study of politics into a natural science. It is as much of a mistake to suppose that the claims of social science should be attacked or defended in the form in which the fetishists of quantitative techniques would like to phrase them. Indeed the use of such techniques to the philosopher of politics might have been more readily apparent if this debate had not been essentially misconceived.

This does not mean that the proper use of such techniques will lead to the formulation of propositions which will of themselves replace the propositions of traditional political theory. It means only that since the prescriptions of political philosophers depend for their usefulness or conviction on their analysis (whether explicit or implicit) of actual political situations, any advance in our knowledge of actual political situations is likely to have important implications for political philosophy. We have seen how this may apply to the studies both of élites and of electors, and it applies just as well to many other topics as to these. It applies also to the type of purely formal or deductive analysis of which the theory of games is the most familiar. Such models or analogues, which are designed only to mirror the behaviour of the real world in terms of a minimum of variables, however unrealistic the assumptions involved, are neither theories nor methods in the ordinary sense. But their use does, as it were, constitute a method (as in the case of Weber's ideal types, which are a kind of model); and they may lead to or even embody satisfactory explanations or theories. It may be that in its application to large-scale problems of politics, as opposed to such specialized fields as the theory of committee decisions, the theory of games has not fulfilled the high hopes which have sometimes been voiced for it. But it has proved interesting enough for the political theorist to be no better able to afford to neglect it than to neglect the would-be general theories or would-be scientific techniques which have been discussed in the earlier part of this chapter.

A good example of such a purely formal analysis remains Professor Kenneth Arrow's *Social Choice and Individual Values* (1951). Arrow is principally concerned with the problem of designing a social welfare function, but this involves a difficulty of direct relevance to what could be called the central problem of all democratic theory: how can we define and give expression to the collective wishes of a community? Arrow's argument shows that our intuitive criteria for democratic decision cannot in fact be satisfied unless we are prepared under certain conditions to accept a social ordering which is either 'imposed' or 'dictatorial'. Put crudely, what Arrow has done is to show that strict democracy is impossible—a result which could hardly be closer to the traditional interest of political philosophers. It may be claimed, of course, that this formal imperfection in the democratic ideal of majority rule is of little or no importance in practice. Or it may be argued that by revising our intuitive criteria for democracy (as several authors have attempted) Arrow's paradox can be circumvented. But Arrow's result is incontrovertible, and to deny that he is dealing with a genuine problem would be absurd. Moreover, results of a similar kind about techniques and strategies of voting do raise issues of obvious importance in the practical working of democratic political systems. A formal analysis of such practices as legislative 'log-rolling' is hardly less relevant to the philosopher of democracy (or oligarchy) than the empirical study of pressure-group techniques. An argument for or against a given system of democracy may have to rest no less on the one than on the other.

The concluding moral remains the same as in all these essays. Even the most successful of formal analogues, or quantitative techniques, or comparative case-studies, or general explanatory theories cannot provide a solution by itself to the questions which philosophers of politics have raised since the time of Plato and Aristotle. How and why the will of the people should be given expression, under what conditions the citizen should or should not obey the State, what are the necessary and sufficient conditions of the just society, are questions whose answer depends ultimately on a philosophical view of the world and of the human beings who live in it. But to argue for any one of the conflicting views which can be held will require the maximum possible reference to our knowledge, whether formal or empirical, about how politics do (or, more important, might under different conditions) work. The attempt to reduce all political philosophy to political science is foredoomed to failure; but the philosopher of politics must be as aware as the political scientist that any attempt to enlarge the scope or application of political science is an attempt worth making.

CHAPTER VII

CLASS, STATUS AND POLITICAL CONFLICT

If we ask the fundamental question—What is the basis of political conflict in a given society?—it is clear that we are straight up against the now familiar problem of choice of terms. The answer will depend not only on the presuppositions underlying the chosen use of the term 'political'; it will also depend on criteria for deciding the relevance or importance of various issues whose impact cannot be positivistically assessed. It is equally clear, however, that the question is not a purely metaphysical one. The ultimate definitions of the terms involved may in a sense be arbitrary, but they can be well or badly justified. Moreover, whatever answer is given will depend on sociological evidence for its justification; it would not, for instance, be hard to dispose of such a suggestion as that religion now constitutes the basis of political conflict in Great Britain. In answering the question, there are in fact two different levels on which it may be rewarding to consider it: first, the sociological (Which groups in a society are the principal competitors for political benefits?); and second, the ideological (What are the principal opposing philosophies of politics?). This raises in turn two further questions central to the discussion of political conflict: first, what are the social groups which we designate as classes? and second, what meaning can most usefully be assigned to the two most overworked terms in the whole political vocabulary, philosophical or sociological—Left and Right?

I want to start by assuming without argument that the principal sociological basis for political conflict in industrialized societies is, in some form, class. This needs some qualifications, and in particular a definition of 'class'. But I think it would be generally agreed by Marxists and non-Marxists alike that except where particular ethnic or religious loyalties override economic interests (or, most divisively of all, coincide with them), this is a reasonable generalization. It only becomes an interesting one, however, when we have offered a more specific analysis of class. Here I want once again to start by following Weber. This is not only because Weber's modification of the Marxian theory on this topic is widely thought more nearly correct, but also on grounds of terminology. Weber's notion is that there is not a single dimension of social stratification, as in Marxist theory, but three. There are good grounds for saying that he is right in this; but even if he is not, it is possible in his terminology to render and compare other theories (including the Marxian). It is not so much that Weber wishes to mean something different from Marx by 'class'. It is rather that he maintains that class, in the Marxian sense of economic class, is not the only dimension of social stratification. He agrees that it is the most important, but he does not agree that the other two dimensions—status and power—can be entirely reduced to it. In particular, we owe to Weber the crucial and still too often neglected distinction between class and status.

Unfortunately, we are at once confronted with a problem in translation. In Weber's vocabulary, the distinction is between *Klassen* and *Stände*, which are normally rendered in English as 'classes' and 'status-groups'. But status-*group* is misleading, in the sense that status-*stratum* would be more accurate; and 'status-stratum' is really too much of a mouthful, even for social scientists. Moreover, *Stände* is the standard German term for 'estates' in the sense of 'estates of the realm', and although estates are (or were) indeed status-strata, the two are by no means interchangeable. The situation is still further complicated when we come to stratification in terms of power. Weber uses the word *Partei*, but what in fact we need is a general term to cover what we mean by factions and pressure-groups as well as what we mean by parties. There are Weber's 'politically oriented corporate groups', but this, like 'status-stratum', is hardly convenient for frequent repetition. The best one can do is probably 'classes', 'status-groups' and 'parties' (or 'power-strata'), leaving the unqualified term 'stratum' for any major sub-division of society to which the vertical metaphors of high and low, top and bottom are appropriate. But it cannot be claimed that the situation in English (or even in German) is very satisfactory.

In Weber's own words, we should speak of classes when 'a number of people have in common a specific component of their opportunities in life insofar as this component is represented exclusively by economic interests in the possession of goods and opportunities for income, and is represented under the conditions of the commodity or labour markets'.[1] Up to this point, Weber's acceptance of the Marxian analysis is clear. But he goes on to say that 'in contrast to the purely economically determined "class-situation" we wish to designate as "status-situation" every typical component of people's fate in life which is determined by a specific social estimation of prestige, whether positive or negative'.[2] It is obvious that class- and status-situation will often coincide. But they will not necessarily: the contrasting types of the impoverished aristocrat and the rejected parvenu are the most familiar, though not the only, examples. Often, of course, status may be seen as a sort of lagged function of class—riches first, status after. Furthermore, it is very possible for status to outlast the class-situation which first enhanced it. But not only is this not always so (contrast, for instance, bookmakers and clergymen), but status may equally act as an independent variable on class-situation. Weber gives a number of historical examples where the status-structure modifies the class-structure by imposing restrictions on the operation of the market. It is, of course, possible at this point to get into historical chicken-and-egg arguments. Indeed, we may follow the contract theorists back to the state of nature where stratification by physical power may have been the primary dimension of the social hierarchy. But irrespective of such Hobbesian fantasies, Weber's distinction can be shown in practice to be both lucid and useful.

To make the distinction more obvious, we may loosely say that class depends on where your money comes from and status on what it goes on: or, as Weber in fact puts it, classes are stratified in terms of production and acquisition of goods, status-groups in terms of consumption. More precisely, the members of your class are those who share your location in the processes of production, distribution and exchange; the members of your status-group are those who share your style of life and your relative position in terms of social estimation and prestige. The difference, once stated, seems self-evident. But much of the trouble is caused by the use of the term 'class' in ordinary language. 'Class' is apt to be used not only as a general term for social stratification but also in contexts where it is in fact status which is meant. To talk about 'working-class' homes or 'middle-class' education or 'U' and 'non-U' speech is to talk about style of life, and therefore status, not about location in the economic hierarchy as such. The two may coincide, but this does not make them the same thing. To make matters worse, academic sociologists have remained surprisingly inconsistent in their vocabulary. When, for example, Professor Marshall says that 'The essence of social class is the way a man is treated by his fellows and, reciprocally, the way he treats them, not the qualities or possessions which cause that treatment',[1] he is giving us a valuable insight on the topic of (in Weberian terms) status. It would be so much more convenient if the multifarious authors on these topics could follow Weber's usage, whether to agree or disagree with him. Some, mercifully, do; but the literature is unnecessarily obscured by a welter of definitions and counter-definitions, discrepancies and tautologies which make it impossible to tell precisely one theory from another, or even whether a given theory is a theory at all. It would be tedious to cite examples. All the reader need do is to sample a few of the now countless textbooks of sociology, as well as more specialized works, where the topic is covered. With rare exceptions, he will find not only a new definition of class explicitly or implicitly put forward; he will also find that the propositions it is used to embody could be adequately rephrased in Weberian terms.[2]

But apart from the terminological confusions of 'class status', 'status class', 'scalar status', 'rank', 'social class', 'economic class' and all the rest, there are, of course, some genuine differences. Most of these can, I have suggested, be expressed in Weberian terms; but some of them are differences not merely about how societies are in fact stratified, but about what it means to speak of any group or potential group or category of people in hierarchical or stratified terms. The most famous example is Marx himself, and his statement in the *Eighteenth Brumaire* about the peasantry: 'In so far as millions of families live under economic conditions of existence that divide their mode of life, their interests and their culture from those of the other classes, and put them in a hostile contrast to the latter, they form a class. In so far as there is merely a local interconnection among these small peasants, and the identity of their interests begets no unity, no national union and no political organization, they do not form a class.'[1] This question, whether classes (or, as it may be, status-groups, or the two together) can be called such if their members are unaware of it themselves may, of course, require an alteration of definition. Marx's nearest approach to a definition is the passage I have just quoted; Weber defines classes not as communities but as 'bases for communal action'; other authors have wanted to speak of classes as 'quasi-groups', 'common interests' and so on. But such genuine differences of definition still do not require us to abandon Weber's delimitation of the dimensions in which stratification (however understood) takes place.

It is, for instance, sometimes said that class represents the objective, and status the subjective element in social stratification. But we can quite well continue to follow Weber, and distinguish both objective and subjective class and status. We can fairly distinguish a person's objective economic situation from what he perceives as his economic situation in the hierarchy; we can also distinguish a person's prestige from what he thinks is his prestige. The first is, in a sense, more objective in that the relevant criterion is more tangible; the second is more subjective in the sense that it depends more on the dispositions of other people. But there is no need to introduce the dangerous terms 'objective' and 'subjective' into our actual definitions. We may simply start from the proposition that all societies are somehow stratified (whatever the categories of stratification should be held to mean) in terms of class, status and power. We can then ask the interesting empirical questions about how closely the three coincide, which depends on what, how far any of them may be minimized, and so on.

There is, however, one important footnote to Weber's analysis of class which deserves separate mention. It becomes most acutely relevant on the topic of white-collar or clerical class-consciousness. In Marxian terms, the clerical worker is as much a proletarian as the coalminer: both are property-less labourers whose living depends on selling their labour under contract. Even in Weberian terms, although the status-situation of the two is different, their class- or market-situation is similar, for they are both similarly placed in terms of their economic opportunities (*Lebenschancen*) under the conditions of the commodity and labour markets. But there is a further difference. As is cogently pointed out by David Lockwood in his study of *The Blackcoated Worker* (1958), we need to distinguish 'market-situation' from 'work-situation', that is, from 'the set of social relationships in which the individual is involved at work by virtue of his position in the division of labour'.[1] This is not a fourth dimension of social stratification, for it is a distinction to be made within stratification by class, not outside of it. But, as Lockwood shows, it takes us a great deal further forward in our understanding of what, to the Marxists, is a notorious case of 'false' consciousness of class, and it is one of the most useful advances in the theory of stratification since Weber himself. It should, moreover, warn us against too simple an explanation either of patterns of political partisanship or of broader changes of occupational and social structure.

The basic distinction, however, between class and status helps us to understand a number of variations in political behaviour. Indeed, the impact of status-deprivation—as opposed to class—on political attitudes can be plausibly traced both in the results of sample surveys and in other historical evidence. Survey evidence from several countries shows that where class (as measured by income) is held constant, those in a higher status-situation (as measured by white-collar as opposed to industrial occupation) are much less likely to vote for parties of the Left. This is no surprise, but it provides a good illustration of the way in which class and status do not wholly coincide. Similarly, it is easily demonstrable that social groups which feel inadequately recognized in terms of status will, even when class is held constant, be more likely to vote for parties of the Left. Ethnic or national minorities provide the readiest examples of this. Michels noticed the radicalism of Jews in Germany before the First World War; and in the United States of today it is well known that Jews are both richer and more likely to vote Democrat than non-Jews in a similar social situation. It requires no great psychological insight to predict that an inferior status-group is likely to resent its position. This will become the more likely the more closed the status-group is (an entirely closed status-group being Weber's useful definition of a caste). For example, economic class makes little difference to the voting behaviour of American Negroes. On a larger scale, it has been argued that the relative importance of status to class in deciding political behaviour depends on the relative prosperity of the country at large: class is more important when times are bad, status when they are good. But, in any case, whether or not large-scale generalizations of this kind can be fully substantiated, they serve once again to make the importance of the distinction clear.

Class, Status and Political Conflict

The muddles which result from neglecting the distinction are perhaps clearest on the topic of the alleged 'deproletarianization' of the British working class and the decline in political or ideological conflict of which this is claimed to be a cause or a symptom. The problem is equally liable to be misunderstood when status is not properly distinguished from economic class, and when status—in the familiar sense of keeping up with the Joneses—is assumed to have overridden class altogether. The processes at work in a changing structure of stratification are in fact exceedingly subtle, and the evidence necessary for their analysis is often difficult if not impossible to obtain. But the necessary prerequisite is a clear conception of just what 'deproletarianization' would consist in. The emphasis on deproletarianization is, in Great Britain at least, largely based on the undoubted increase in the prosperity of the working class and the perpetuation by the British electorate of more than ten years of Conservative rule. But a bigger pay-packet does not automatically confer on a working-class man either the attitudes, or the speech, or the dress, or the recognition as an equal, of a different status-group. To assume, as some commentators seem to do, that whenever a factory worker buys a spin drier or stops wearing a cloth cap or fails to vote Labour at a parliamentary election he is therefore motivated by the quest for status at the expense of traditional class loyalties is frankly absurd. David Lockwood has once again made the essential point: 'A washing-machine', as he puts it, 'is a washing-machine is a washing-machine.'[1]

We in fact know remarkably little about the conditions necessary for a large-scale readjustment of the status hierarchy, let alone about the patterns of political allegiance which might emerge from it. There is good evidence to show that an improvement in economic conditions, though it may be a necessary condition for a realignment of status, is not a sufficient condition: patterns of relationships, loyalties and underlying social attitudes characteristic of the 'traditional' working class may well outlast the incursions of affluence. Moreover, even persistently high wages do not alter the basic market-situation of the manual worker; he remains virtually property-less even in prosperity. But what are the sufficient conditions for realignment of status? And can it ever reach the point where we shall regularly see the charge-hand and the managing director sitting down to dinner together at the Conservative Club or in each other's homes?

There are several possible ways in which status mobility might operate: according to one theory, economic mobility leads to the adoption of a non-proletarian style of life and this may lead in turn to social relationships with status-groups drawn from the middle class; according to another theory, the crucial process is, in the American term, 'anticipatory socialization' whereby a normative aspiration to a different status-group precedes and motivates the acquisition of whatever is needed in order to assimilate to it; yet another view is that working-class prosperity breaks the two main status-groups of proletariat and bourgeoisie into three—traditional proletarians, traditional bourgeois and a self-conscious middle group (perhaps of potential Liberal voters) drawn economically from the top of the manual and the bottom of the non-manual classes. But the evidence needed to choose among these theories is still lacking. The stage has only just been reached of knowing what questions need to be asked.

Moreover, there is a diversity of factors involved apart from the economic habits of prosperity. Work-situation, in Lockwood's sense, is obviously one of these. So is the social composition and even geographical layout of the district where a given family lives. In addition, there may be the effects of the third dimension of stratification—power. A union official may rise in the power hierarchy before either altering his style of life or necessarily greatly improving his economic position. But how, for instance, does he bring up his children after his knighthood? Or what sort of person does he want his daughter to marry? All these questions can only be settled by evidence of which we still have very little. We know something about the social conditions on council estates and in new towns; we know something about the sorts of manual workers who vote Conservative and those (not necessarily the same) who describe themselves to interviewers as 'middle-class'; we know something about the effects of work-situation on proletarian attitudes and loyalties. But exactly how the social structure is altering in terms of overall patterns of stratification we are not yet equipped to describe, let alone to explain. Nor can any diagnosis of the effect of these changes on the long-term trends of national politics be more than tentative and conditional. What has first to be done is to phrase the interesting questions; and these, I have suggested, can best be put (however they will be answered) in a modified form of the terms laid down by Weber as the basic dimensions of social stratification.

The need to make the right distinctions and to phrase the right questions is, if anything, still more acute when we come to discuss such issues as these in the traditional terms of Left and Right. It is, after all, a historical accident to which we owe these terms; if the deputies in the French Revolutionary assembly had not seated themselves as they did, the political vocabulary of Europe and of most of the world would have been markedly different. Some commentators, appalled at the degree of ambiguity with which these terms have come to be bandied about, have argued that we should do better to abolish them altogether. But even if this is true, the terms are now so deeply imbedded into our mode of political thinking that the recommendation stands no chance of being effectively put into practice. All that can be done, therefore, is to ask how the terms should best be used.

It has to be conceded at the outset that there are some political situations where to talk of Left and Right is wholly inappropriate or even meaningless. This is the case for many periods even of Western European history. It is even more the case for the types of societies described by the political anthropologists where, as we saw in Chapter II, we must be prepared to talk of 'stateless societies' if we are to retain for the notion of 'state' its recommended meaning. It is, despite this, still possible to retain for such societies Weber's terminology of stratification, if only to describe how little they are by European standards stratified. But notions of Left and Right are totally irrelevant. By way of illustration, it is worth quoting a paragraph from perhaps the best-known description of one of these societies—the description of the Tallensi of Northern Ghana (as they were prior to 1934) which is given by Professor Fortes.

'Economically, therefore,' says Fortes, 'the Tallensi are a homogeneous, sedentary, equalitarian peasantry. Every settlement has a few men of more than average wealth, due usually to the fact that they have many sons to farm for them. But no social privileges attach to wealth, though it is admired and envied. Wealth cannot be accumulated. It is partly utilized to add to the number of wives in the joint family, thus progressively increasing the drain on its resources, and is eventually distributed by inheritance. Thus

Class, Status and Political Conflict

it has only a temporary advantage. There are no economic classes cutting across and detracting from the solidarity of lineage, clan and local community, a fact of utmost importance for the political organization.'[1]

The Tallensi were not without any political organization whatever. But they were without a centralized State, and, as we have just learnt, without classes. We must therefore say of them that they had no class hierarchy except that larger families might be slightly more prosperous; they had a status hierarchy, but wealth played a much less important part in it than factors determined by the lineage system; they had no universal power hierarchy, since they had no centralized authority, but there was a hierarchy of power within the equivalent segments which was governed by kinship and seniority and upheld by established sanctions. There was thus a situation in which the notion of the state was irrelevant, stratification more or less minimal, and the terms Left and Right devoid of any tangible meaning at all. This is an extreme case. But it serves as a reminder that not very much of our sociological or political vocabulary is of universal application. This does not mean that we should feel any less free to use our terms when they do apply. But the recurrent problem is to make sure that they do.

Even when we turn to the industrialized and sophisticated societies where Left and Right have the readiest application, we have still to be careful; and perhaps the first precaution is to distinguish any useful sense of Left and Right from the wholly separate dimension of extremism. Whether totalitarianism is really as new a historical phenomenon as some of its analysts (such as Miss Arendt) have argued is yet a further question which I do not mean to enter into. But the history of Germany and Soviet Russia in the twentieth century has shown us, on any interpretation, that the extremes of totalitarian coercion are the monopoly neither of the far Left nor of the far Right. It may be that the totalitarian element of both is their most significant and also their most unpleasant feature; but there is nothing by definition more extremist about one than the other. To live in, Stalin's Russia may have felt more like Hitler's Germany than a parliamentary regime of either Left or Right feels like either. But this does not oblige us to say that totalitarianism of the Left and Right are identical, either sociologically or ideologically. To argue, as an American political scientist has recently done, that 'the fact is that Stalinism was essentially identical with Hitlerism and the other expressions of Fascism'[1] is to blur for the sake of one important similarity two equally important differences.

Let me first of all take the ideological difference. There are several ideological issues which cut across the conventional Left–Right spectrum, and I shall come back in a moment to the most important of these. But the distinction in political philosophy—however much the practices of those who profess such philosophies may fall short of their professions —is a fundamental one. It is, indeed, a distinction between two opposite and irreconcilable views of the nature of man. This point has been well made by Professor Talmon in his study of *The Origins of Totalitarian Democracy*.[2] Talmon, however, makes a double distinction, whereas I think his conclusion may be rephrased into a single fundamental difference. To the Left, men are by nature endowed with an ultimate equality in natural virtue; to the Right, they are not. From these different pictures of man as essentially good and essentially bad spring both the anarchism of the Left and the racism of the Right, the Left's ideal of a community of free men and the Right's ideal of the communal hierarchy of the nation-state, the Left's voluminous Utopianism and the Right's anti-intellectualist irrationalism.

It is true that Lenin—to take only the most obvious example—was in his way as much of an élitist as any ruler or theoretician of the Right. But numerous passages can be quoted from his writings to show his belief that an élite is only necessary because imperfect institutions have perverted men from their natural goodness. This is the anarchist strain which we have already noticed running through to Lenin from Saint-Simon, but appearing in different versions in writers as diverse as Paine, Godwin, Babeuf, Owen, Fourier, Proudhon and Marx himself (though it was Engels who actually coined the famous phrase about the 'withering away' of the State). Government, on this theory, is not merely the badge of lost innocence; it is the not immovable barrier to a state of innocence which, whether once lost or never in historical fact attained, will in the end find a lasting fulfilment. When, therefore, the Left resorts to coercion, it is only to hasten the advent of the promised paradise. When the Right resorts to coercion, it is part of the natural order of things; it is a way (to quote Professor Talmon) 'of maintaining order among poor and unruly creatures, and training them to act in a manner alien to their mediocre nature'.

The sociological distinction, however, between Left and Right is a different matter altogether—basically, it is nothing other than the perennial argument between the poor and the rich. But we can put it a little more precisely. Given a population which we can arrange by class along a rough continuum from the proletariat at one end through the artisans, farmers, shopkeepers and professional men to the big landowners and industrialists at the other end, we can then ask the question: to which group do different parties or movements appeal and draw from them in return their principal support?

One of the most interesting analyses of this is an essay by Professor Lipset entitled 'Fascism—Left, Right and Center'.[1] On the basis of voting statistics and survey data, Lipset argues that different extremist movements too glibly labelled 'Fascist' have in fact drawn their support from very different social classes. One of his best examples is Peronism. Peronism used generally to be labelled as a Fascist movement; but in sociological terms it was not a Fascism of the Right. Peron drew his support from the trade unions, the urban workers and the landless rural proletariat. He was opposed by the industrialists, the landlords and the middle class. When he was brought down, it was from the Right—by the army and the Church. His electoral majorities (which there is no need to suppose were not genuine) came from people who would otherwise have voted not for the Right, but for Socialist or even Communist parties.

Similarly, Lipset shows in the German case how support for Nazism was initially based not—as the Marxists would have it—on the far Right, but on the middle class. Although the period of Hitler's rise to power is too early for sample-survey data, Lipset is able to support his argument both by an ecological analysis and by tracing the fortunes of the separate parties. The Nazis gained most in areas where the traditional Right was in any case weakest, so that it can hardly be from the traditional Right that they drew their main support. Moreover, the parties whose support declined most sharply as the Nazis increased their gains were the parties appealing explicitly to the petty middle class—shopkeepers, small farmers and self-employed artisans. It used to be argued that Hitler's success was due to the sup-

Class, Status and Political Conflict

port of the hitherto apathetic. But although many of these did vote for Hitler—particularly among the unemployed—they did so in large numbers only at a relatively late stage. Similarly, it is quite true that Hitler later came to be supported by big business and the industrialists. But this was much less true at the outset. Sociologically, Nazism was an extremism of the middle class.

But the ideological distinction still holds good, Lipset's analysis notwithstanding. Thus, Peronism was ideologically very much of the Right. It was nationalistic, militaristic and élitist, and Peron on occasion praised both Mussolini and Hitler. In a sense, therefore, Peronism could be labelled a Rightism of the Left, whereas the Rightism of the Right would be represented rather by Salazar's Portugal or Horthy's Hungary where the regime is (or was) in sociological terms based on those interests most concerned to maintain the *status quo*. Equally, it would be conceivable to have a party exemplifying a Leftism of the Right as opposed to a Leftism based on the traditionally underprivileged classes. The Fabians might do as an example; or a party consisting, as it were, of Tolstoy and friends would have to be described in some such terms. The ideological and sociological senses of Left and Right will very often coincide, but they need not necessarily do so. The terms are worth retaining if only because it would be so difficult to get rid of them; but if they are to remain useful, then this distinction has to be kept clear.

Finally, however, let me say something about the most important distinction which cuts across any ideological definition of the Left–Right spectrum—the distinction expressed in the German terms *Gemeinschaft* and *Gesellschaft*. The canonical exposition of these terms is the work by Ferdinand Tönnies which takes them as its title and which was first published in 1887. But they embody a distinction which in one form or another can be traced back to Plato and Aristotle. The English translation of Tönnies's work is *Community and Association*, but these words are so hopelessly ambiguous without a good deal of further qualification that it is undoubtedly better to take the German as it stands. The distinction expressed is intuitively a fairly obvious one. There is on the one hand the small, organic, pre-industrial, close-knit status society (*Gemeinschaft*); on the other, there is the big, impersonal, industrialized, bureaucratic contract society (*Gesellschaft*). Of course, not all the elements of each ideal type need ever go together. But the distinction, though both commonplace and imprecise, is exceedingly important both to the sociology and to the philosophy of politics.

The issue is neither whether man is ultimately perfectible nor whether the rich are too rich as compared to the poor. It is rather a question of which of two incompatible sets of organizational virtues should be preferred. This is a problem irrespective of which social groups or strata are the principal recipients of economic or political benefits. Although the *Gemeinschaft* type is more suggestive of organic feudalism and the *Gesellschaft* type of atomistic capitalism, there is in principle no reason why a *Gemeinschaft* society may not (like the Tallensi) be egalitarian or a *Gesellschaft* society aristocratic. The distinction is more nearly embodied in the overtones, whether good or bad, of 'civilization'. On one side are the simple virtues (or are they vices?) of the proverbial village community; on the other are the benefits (or are they merely illusory benefits?) of the big, bustling city. If we realign the traditional political theorists on the basis of this one issue, then there are some startling alliances across the Left–Right line, for William

Class, Status and Political Conflict

Morris must be bracketed with Burke, and Bentham with Stalin. The problem is partly the same as the one which underlies Marx's worries about 'alienation' and Weber's about 'disenchantment' and 'rationalization'. As both Marx and Weber were sharply aware, history can be seen in terms of a progress from *Gemeinschaft* to *Gesellschaft*. This enables the question to be put more crudely still: how can we have the advantages without the disadvantages of progress?

The question obtrudes itself most forcibly in the context of industrialization, and it remains just as difficult to those now concerned with the problems of the underdeveloped countries as it was to Marx or Weber or Durkheim. Given the irreversible fact of an industrial revolution, should its ill-effects be modified or counteracted by preserving the folk-type social bonds? Or should rationalization, however painful for the moment, be carried through to its logical conclusion and society turned into a harmonious and efficient machine? We are concerned not simply with distribution of benefits, but with the fundamental nature of all the social relationships—economic, familial, religious, political—which go to make up the totality of a society. The alternative patterns of *Gemeinschaft* and *Gesellschaft* are not compatible. We cannot have all the advantages of centralization at the same time as all the advantages of face-to-face relationships. There is an unavoidable conflict between the bureaucratic efficiency of which Weber is the classical analyst and a full regard for individual and separate claims. Moreover, there is the problem as old as Plato's myths of how to find substitutes for the traditional beliefs and mores which hold a *Gemeinschaft* society together: 'the essential condition', said Al Ghazali a very long time before Weber, 'in the holder of a traditional faith is that he should not know he is a traditionalist'. Saint-Simon and Comte proposed to remedy this aspect of the problem by creating an artificial 'religion of humanity'; but Al Ghazali's observation is really much more to the point. We have to choose between two organizational blueprints for society, both of which are comprehensive, but can only to a very limited degree be reconciled with each other. It is not a choice between Left and Right in either or any of their senses; it is more, as it were, a choice between rationalization and fellowship. Which, therefore, should we be trying to emphasize?

If we are to answer this question, it is clear that we need not only the *a priori* philosophers but also sociologists from many of the different branches of social science. Any prescriptive theory on these topics needs to be supported by sociological evidence; but, equally, no amount of sociological generalization, however firmly established, can alone provide the answer. Weber at one point declares that social science can never prove to people what they ought to do but only what they can and (sometimes) what they want to do. In a sense, this is quite true. But Weber himself has shown that the social scientist must be a philosopher, whether he wants to or not; and to imply that all philosophies are arbitrary and immune to adjudication is (as I shall try to show in my last chapter) demonstrably false. If there is to be any workable resolution of the questions disputed between the partisans of Left and Right, *Gemeinschaft* and *Gesellschaft*, there are needed both political philosophers with knowledge of social science and political sociologists with a grasp of philosophy. Perhaps these come to the same thing. Indeed, the examples of Marx and even Weber (despite his dichotomy of fact and value) are enough to demonstrate it. But, ironically enough, it is Weber, whose discussion of these topics I have so much relied on, who has been partly responsible for the separation of political philosophy and political sociology which I have argued that we should try to remedy. It is a good thing that the practitioners of both should be aware of the distinction; it is a pity if such an awareness should impel them into trying to keep the two as far apart as possible.

CHAPTER VIII

SOCIAL SCIENCE AND POLITICAL THEORY

In a speech which he delivered at the University of Munich two years before his death, Weber quotes with approval from Tolstoy: 'Science is meaningless because it gives no answer to our question, the only question important to us: "What shall we do and how shall we live?"'; and Weber goes on to say: 'That science does not give an answer to this is indisputable.'[1] To Weber, academic knowledge can never enable us to interpret the meaning of the world; at best, it can only force us to clarify the *Weltanschauung* which underlies our own particular interpretation. Such interpretations are essentially arbitrary, and where they conflict there is nothing more to be said: each person must follow his own. In a sense, of course, Weber is obviously right. To take one of his own examples, no amount of historical research is going to make a Catholic and a Freemason agree in their interpretation of religious history. Moreover, Weber was very properly concerned, in his writings on method, to attack the lecture-room moralists whose social science is no more than a gloss of counterfeit objectivity used to disguise their sermons and prejudices. But he ends up in a position very similar to that put forward in T. D. Weldon's notorious *Vocabulary of Politics* (1953). A political philosophy, to Weber almost as much as to Weldon, is like a taste for ice-cream. One can only state one's taste and go away—there is no point in arguing.

On this point, I want to argue that Weber is wrong—not,

perhaps, entirely wrong, but wrong enough for us to need to make one major qualification to his argument. We have already seen that we must modify Weber's dichotomy between sociological questions and the procedures for answering them, which is itself closely tied to his dichotomy between value and fact. But this is not yet enough to impugn his claim that evaluative standpoints are immune to argument. His own discussion has shown both that an evaluative element enters into the most rigorous social science and also that the feasibility of putting an evaluation or prescription into practice will depend on sociological evidence for its assessment. But to establish that the different standpoints or *Weltanschauungen* which we are free to choose from are not all equally arbitrary and at some basic point unarguable, a separate argument is needed of a purely philosophical kind.

In an essay on 'The Meaning of Ethical Neutrality in Sociology and Economics'[1] Weber sets out a classification of the ways in which he thinks that meaningful argument is possible on questions of value. You can, he says, assess the logical consistency of a set of value-axioms; or you can argue about whether what follows from such axioms is relevant to the case at hand; or you can discuss the consequences which would follow in practice from the implementation of such axioms. All such discussion, says Weber, is likely to be useful and may oblige one or other of the disputants to modify his position. Moreover, such discussion may also be important in leading to the selection of particular problems for empirical investigation. But none of this implies any modification of Weber's dichotomy between fact and value. He still maintains as stoutly as Hume before him or Weldon since that you cannot jump from an 'is' to an 'ought'.

Weber gives as his example of an unarguable position that of an extreme syndicalist for whom no consideration of the feasibility or consequences of his actions is relevant. A certain course of action is assigned by him an overriding value, and there is nothing more to be said. But if we examine such a case more closely, we see that it implies a distinction which Weber's own notions of arguability should take account of—the distinction (if we are careful about the use of these dangerous terms) between reasonable and unreasonable disputants.

Let us suppose that we are confronted with Weber's syndicalist. What we shall be wise to do is not merely to ask for a statement of his political philosophy and then state our own disagreement with it, but to ask the further question, whatever he replies, 'Why do you believe that?'. Weber seems to imply that his syndicalist neither will nor needs to do more than to reassert that he believes what he believes because he does. But consider what is likely to happen in practice. The syndicalist might give as the first axiom of his political philosophy the assertion that all centralized government must be resisted by force, whatever the suffering caused and however unlikely the expectation of success. When we ask him why he believes this, it may be that we shall get no further: he may say only that he feels an intuitive certainty that he should act in this way, that he simply *knows* that his view is the right one. But if this is all that he is prepared to say, then we shall suggest to him that there is no more reason why we should accept his views than those of a person who believes that it is the duty of the government to execute all widows and orphans. If, at this point, the syndicalist is to make any kind of move to justify his position, then he will have to make some such reply as that he believes all government to be evil. But as soon as he does this, we shall ask him for evidence; and we shall thereby have embarked on just such a political-sociological discussion as may require him to modify his position. Weber might say, of course, that he has in mind the person who still refuses to modify his syndicalist beliefs whatever hypothetical evidence we could bring against them. But if he can give no reason at all, we are entitled to bracket him with the man who proposes that widows and orphans should be killed for no other reason than that they are widows and orphans.

To the thorough-going sceptic, of course, this sort of example makes no difference, for he will refuse (or pretend to refuse) to allow that any statement of a political belief is more unreasonable, or irrational, or arbitrary than any other. He will claim that a belief that the State should execute widows and orphans is no more easily dismissed than a claim that pensions should be provided for them, since both can be reduced to what we may call the 'Weldon model' of liking or not liking ice-cream. But even in the lecture-rooms of the metaphysicians, where we are required to start by doubting everything, it is difficult to believe anyone who claims to take this claim entirely seriously. Furthermore, there is an ingenious philosophical argument which can be enlisted in order to counter such people on their own ground. For what we can require them to do is to advance a criterion of their own for distinguishing between scepticisms. If they adopt some kind of total solipsism, then they have no business to be interested in either the philosophy or the sociology of politics anyway. But if—which we can surely start our discussion by assuming—they are prepared to forgo a professional doubt about the evidence of their senses or of natural science, then we may attack them with their own weapons. Weber, for instance, is far from being a total sceptic. As we have several times had occasion to emphasize, his stress on the scientific objectivity which he prescribes for the conduct of a sociological investigation involves of itself an unsceptical and 'value-relevant' *Gesichtspunkt*. Why, therefore, does he feel obliged to insist that all *Weltanschauungen* (which must include his own) are unarguable and arbitrary?

The principal argument which the sceptic puts forward is usually to point to the indisputable variety of political and ethical beliefs and the lack of any universally accepted criterion for distinguishing between them. But this is not in fact the point. Our belief in the results of natural science does not rest on the majority principle—why, therefore, should our beliefs about politics? No matter how many people are recruited to the flat-earthers, those who believe the earth to be more or less of a sphere will not for that reason alone feel obliged to change their minds. I can conceive of a situation in which I might be brought to doubt my conviction that the earth is not flat, but it would arise only as a result of scientific arguments presented to me showing why the alleged demonstrations of its roundness came to be mistakenly accepted as correct. In the same way, it is not the simple diversity of political beliefs which need compel us to the conclusion that every point of view should be accorded equal treatment. Unless we are prepared also to be sceptical about those same standards of scientific objectivity which Weber himself enjoins, we are not *a priori* debarred from ruling out some of the limitlessly conceivable *Weltanschauungen* with the same readiness that we are prepared to rule out the flat-earthers' explanation of circumnavigation.

This does not, however, by any means solve the whole problem, for there are many cases such as Weber may have in mind and which in fact support his argument far better than his syndicalist example. These are the cases in which the advocate of a given viewpoint has an entirely coherent answer, embracing all the available evidence, to our question 'why do you believe that?'. There may be, in such cases, a kind of immunity to argument which cannot be dismissed as 'irrational' in at all the same sense of that word which was just now applied to the would-be killer of widows and orphans. Marxism, in some at least of its many variants, is the most obvious example. Not only does it provide a framework which can be guaranteed in advance to cover whatever evidence the empirical sociologist of politics may produce, but it can also be guaranteed to provide a self-confirming interpretation of what has induced its opponents to reject it. The same is true of doctrinaire Freudianism, and (as put forward by some of its believers) Roman Catholicism. Not only may the holders of such doctrines remain undismayed either by being required to specify why they hold to them or by being questioned on the grounds of feasibility and consistency which are all that Weber is prepared to allow; they can also show why a disbeliever's reluctance to accept their doctrines is a further demonstration of their validity.

A disbelief in Marxism results from that same influence of economic forces and factors which Marxism has so effectively exposed; a disbelief in Freudianism results from the same internal resistances which Freud showed to be characteristic of those who best exemplify his diagnoses; a disbelief in Catholicism results from a state of sin which only a willingness to accept the grace of God will enable the sinner to overcome. The last case is, perhaps, significantly different from the other two in that an element of pure 'faith' is generally stipulated as a precondition for the acceptance of Catholicism. But as far as arguability is concerned, this is a less significant difference than might appear. It is what is sometimes described as the 'closed' character of all three systems which renders them immune to evidence in the way that a theory in the natural sciences never can be. It is not that the holder of such a belief may never change his mind, but that if he does the process is better described by such terms as 'conversion' than by either the ice-cream model ('he decided he didn't like it after all') or the natural-science model ('his evidence failed to confirm his hypothesis').

At this point, another line of argument becomes directly relevant, namely the propositions of what is now generally known as the sociology of knowledge. The study as we now understand it was founded by Marx, although it is hinted at by Saint-Simon and Comte. Its general thesis, whether it takes a Marxian or a non-Marxian form, is that what is held to be true in a given society at a given time is the determined product of the economic or social conditions at work in that society. But the problem which this immediately raises is that if all knowledge is relative to its time and place then so is the knowledge that this proposition is itself true. To say that historical materialism, for instance, is objectively valid because it is the doctrine whereby the subjective or socially determined element in all doctrines may be allowed for, still does not enable us to break out of the regress. Why should the doctrine that all doctrines are relative not be relative itself? The effort to cope with this problem and those which follow from it has led a succession of authors into some very complicated logical contortions necessary to keep them walking, as it were, on the waters of a bottomless relativism. Of these authors, the two most notable are Lukacs and Karl Mannheim.

Lukacs is of all the Marxist sociologists the most subtle,

though he is also the least orthodox. I have already referred *à propos* of Marx himself to the way in which Lukacs was attacked for being insufficiently materialist. But his argument remains much the most ingenious (though still ultimately unsuccessful) of those which set out to locate the perception of objective truth in the proletarian class-consciousness. It involves a skilful amalgam of philosophical and sociological considerations. Lukacs is fully aware of the counterclaim that historical materialism may be turned against itself. But he argues that the proletarian viewpoint can be shown superior to the bourgeois, because unlike the bourgeois it incorporates the totality of the evolving historical process. All viewpoints are historically conditioned; but that this is true of the right one as well as the wrong one does not make the right one any less correct. On the contrary, argues Lukacs, it is the historically conditioned vantage-point of the proletariat which is precisely what enables it to evolve a doctrine which comprehends its own situation and that of the bourgeoisie far better than the 'false consciousness' of the bourgeoisie whose causes and effects can be sociologically and historically demonstrated.

Lukacs's argument is exceedingly ingenious. But it will not quite do, for it is still not adequate to the objection that the proletariat's view need not be final. Why will not the proletariat's class-consciousness (and therefore its vision of objective historical truth) change as the history of which the proletariat is a part also changes? The vindication of the proletariat's present view, and the guide to action which this view entails, can only be accomplished by an appeal to an argument derived from outside the historical context which has produced it. Lukacs's attempt to do just this—which can be labelled a Hegelian attempt, if the term is useful—is both the strength and the weakness of his argument. He has to assign a prior and objective truth to historical materialism, just as he is prepared to say that Copernican astronomy was right before Copernicus.[1] But this cannot be made quite consistent with the relativism disclosed by historical materialism according to which even bourgeois astronomy (and why not, therefore, historical materialism itself?) is only the product of a given period and part of the self-serving ideology of a given economic class. Historical materialism, even as expounded by Lukacs, still cannot be immunized against the charge of relativizing itself as well.

Mannheim's answer owes something to Lukacs, but rests ultimately on less Marxian (or, one might say, less proletarian) grounds. Mannheim is inconsistent to the point of muddle, but he does propose a kind of solution. It lies in transferring, as it were, Lukacs's proletarian vantage-point to the intelligentsia, to what he calls the 'unanchored, *relatively* classless stratum'[2] which can from an unprejudiced social situation assess and synthesize the various viewpoints whose social origins can be determined and analysed. But this will not do either. In the first place, the objection can be made (as, for that matter, it also can against Lukacs) that it is illegitimate to talk of classes as having opinions or ideas; it is individual members of classes who have opinions and ideas, and intellectuals or proletarians can be only too easily observed to disagree with each other about precisely those topics on which Lukacs and Mannheim assign to them an ideal-typical unanimity. Secondly, there is no reason why the pragmatic impartiality of Mannheim's intellectual might not lead him into errors just as much as might a commitment to one or other class. His unattachment is just as much a product of social forces—a point which is emphasized by Mannheim's explicit contrast with a priestly intelligentsia—and there is no reason

Social Science and Political Theory

why a principle of reconciling opposites should not produce a mistaken attempt at compromise just as much as an ideally eclectic synthesis. Thirdly, Mannheim gives no rule for just how his intellectuals are to achieve their sensible synthesis. As Professor Merton caustically observes, Mannheim's attempts to rely on the classless intellectual (by implication, Mannheim himself) to rescue him from relativism are like nothing so much as Baron Munchausen's feat of extricating himself from a swamp by pulling on his whiskers.[1]

In the face of these failures to resolve the fundamental dilemma of relativism, the conclusion to be drawn is surely that even the most ingenious answers will prove inadequate when it is the wrong question which is being asked. The sociology of knowledge is immensely rewarding as a field of historical and anthropological study. The thesis that the canons of scientific objectivity are themselves the product of uniquely Western social conditions is a fascinating one not only to the historian of science as such. Why was it the Greeks who discovered the concept, and the Renaissance the experiment?[2] What determines when and where technological discoveries are made and, if made, implemented? And so on. But to look to the sociology of knowledge for the single *Gesichtspunkt* to which, on its own analysis, a wholly objective validity can be assigned is as mistaken as to look to a physicist (though this is sometimes done) for adjudication of the ontological proof of the existence of God. There is no answer to the question as formulated by Lukacs, or Mannheim, or Scheler, or Durkheim (who puts forward a kind of sociology of knowledge in the concluding chapter of *The Elementary Forms of the Religious Life*). To make the nature of the problem clear we shall have to look at it from a slightly different point of view. For this purpose, it will be convenient to go back to Weber, and to a crucial distinction which underlies his argument on this topic.

We must begin with the categorical assertion that the source of a belief is logically irrelevant to its validity, whatever criteria of validity are involved. It does not matter if Weber wrote *The Protestant Ethic and the Spirit of Capitalism* out of the desire to controvert dialectical materialism any more than it matters whether Machiavelli wrote *The Prince* in the hope of getting office from the Medici. The question is only whether the conclusion is right or wrong; and provided we are prepared simply to ignore the sceptic who wishes to deny meaning to these two terms in any context whatever, then by whatever criterion of truth is chosen, the truth of a proposition can be assessed quite independently of how it happened to be arrived at. It is here that we must make Weber's distinction. As he emphasizes, any choice of vocabulary or conceptual framework entails an evaluation. If, therefore, a given vocabulary is, as it must be, in some sense the product of the culture and historical circumstances in which it arose, then to explain just how it came to be the product may elucidate the evaluation involved but cannot mitigate or diminish it. It may be possible to show how the economics of Adam Smith and Ricardo were the product of their bourgeois culture, and also to reinterpret their conclusions in the light of a later and perhaps more sophisticated conceptual framework than they had available to them. But the fact remains that they did not have available to them the vocabulary of Marshall or Keynes. We may test their conclusions by the same standards of objectivity as we test the conclusions of Keynes; but it is irrelevant to dismiss them as 'wrong' on the sole ground that their conclusions are circumscribed by a vocabulary which we believe can be improved upon.

This is the point of Weber's distinction. An author cannot be criticized because his *Gesichtspunkt* is, like every other, socially conditioned and 'value-relevant'; but what can nevertheless be required from him is *Unbefangenheit*, or freedom from prejudice—a word which, significantly enough, Lukacs himself is prepared to apply to the economics of Smith and Ricardo.[1] The distinction is between an 'ideology' in the neutral, almost Kantian sense of conceptual categories which it would be inconceivable to do without, and 'ideology' in the sense of an interest-serving doctrine put forward for an ulterior end. Put more crudely, the distinction is between believing what you cannot help thinking is true and believing what you want to think is true.

There may, of course, be a considerable usefulness *ad hominem* in the accusation that someone believes a doctrine because it suits his needs or interests to do so. Moreover, the argument from social conditioning may have a precautionary function, for it may help to show just how much of a particular doctrine is not susceptible to empirical argument. But it is not strictly relevant to our problem, which is the other kind, as it were, of ideology or evaluation. Given that, as Weber requires, a man is consistent and honest in terms of his own *Gesichtspunkt*, and that he is able within his framework to incorporate without evasion or illogicality any evidence which might have a bearing upon it, must we still treat all such guiding points of view, however much or little they are socially conditioned, as equally immune to argument?

I have already suggested that we have an *ad hominem* argument against Weber on this topic, for we can challenge him to be as sceptical of his methodological precepts as he is in principle of the *Weltanschauung* which underlies them. But this does not carry the argument any farther forward.

What we must do instead is to return to the argument that we can, after all, make some evaluation as between *Weltanschauungen* themselves. We have seen that their diversity is no obstacle by itself, and we have also seen that Weber's own argument of an intractable syndicalist may be used against him. Whatever philosophy of politics a person puts forward, we may ask him for his reasons for believing it; and some responses—or, more accurately, lack of responses—may be at least as confidently dismissed from our discussion as the flat-earthers from planning the programme of research for the next International Geophysical Year. The difficult question is how much farther we can go than this.

The sceptic will still try to claim that all political philosophies can be ultimately reduced to the ice-cream model. But despite this claim, there are strong arguments to the effect that there is a shared body of political-philosophical beliefs which may be treated as analogous to the starting-point for belief in the canons of natural science. Disputes, of course, will still be possible (as they are among natural scientists). But all political philosophies, however different, which need to be taken seriously can still be claimed to rest on a certain basis of accepted premises. In addition to this, I want to argue that although Weber is right in saying that disputes between rival political philosophies are likely beyond a certain point to be unresolvable—particularly in the case of the sort of closed and coherent systems which I touched on earlier—it would still be a mistake to argue that they can be shown necessarily incapable of ever being resolved. Moreover, the effort to resolve them will involve an appeal not only to the philosophers but also to the sociologists of politics.

The first part of this thesis I want to rest not on any argument of my own, but on the book which I believe to be

Social Science and Political Theory

the most relevant to this issue to have appeared for a long time: Professor Hart's *The Concept of Law* (1961). The book is, as its title suggests, principally intended for the student of jurisprudence. But, for the present argument, its most important section is two chapters entitled 'Justice and Morality' and 'Laws and Morals', and in particular Hart's arguments for what he is explicitly prepared to call the 'minimum content of natural law'. 'It is a truth', he remarks, 'of some importance that for the adequate description not only of law but of many other social institutions, a place must be reserved, besides definitions and ordinary statements of fact, for a third category of statements: those the truth of which is contingent on human beings and the world they live in retaining the salient characteristics which they have.'[1] What this means is that unless we wish to disregard those principles without which social life would not be possible at all, then we may list a set of assertions which are best described, with Hart, as the minimum content of natural law. Hart lists five particular truisms which provide the basis for such a set of assertions: human vulnerability, approximate equality, limited altruism, limited resources, and limited understanding and strength of will. Because of these facts, which Hart emphasizes to be contingent facts, there are certain rules or principles which must be embodied in any social organization which is to be viable. Of course, it can always be argued that there may be political philosophies which deny the value of social organization altogether or which set up the life of the hermit as the only and overriding ideal. But it is surely reasonable, with Hart, to dismiss such notions without argument; we need no more take seriously the political philosophy of (to take Hart's own example) a suicide club than we did the flat-earthers' geography.

Moreover, if we look at the grounds on which political philosophies are recommended by their authors, we see that there are certain minimal ends which they all claim to be showing mankind how to attain. No political philosopher has ever suggested that suffering should be maximized, or that it is the duty of the State to take measures ensuring that contracts and promises are never kept. This does not mean that all political philosophies are simply different recommendations of the most efficient means to agreed ends. It does mean, however, that certain minimum ends are agreed upon, and that it is only beyond this point that we shall be confronted with disagreements where Weber's argument comes into its own.

Perhaps the best example of these more difficult disagreements is the notion of social justice, which Weber does at one point refer to. There is here a proverbial conflict between deserts and needs as the criterion for the allocation of communal resources, and this conflict is irreconcilable by any single ethical norm. The two points of view are epitomized in Weber's own discussion by Schmoller and Babeuf. If we were to set these two to arguing, and provide them with any evidence that they might require, it could be safely predicted that they would continue to disagree no matter how much discussion of feasibility and consistency they had gone through. They would both, one may assume, subscribe to Hart's version of natural law; but this would be no help whatever in dealing with just those further questions where the difference between them would be found to be most acute.

Weber implies, of course, that there is nothing more to be done. But I think it can be claimed that he is wrong. We have already referred to the fact that even Marxists and Catholics, or Syndicalists and Freemasons, have been known to change their minds. Although the process is better described as 'loss of belief' than as 'acceptance of an alternative hypothesis', it still involves a 'change of mind' in the ordinary sense of that term—a sense exclusive, that is to say, of changes artificially induced by drugs or surgery. There may, of course, be psychological factors at work in any given case which predispose a person to being unwilling or even unable to surrender the beliefs from which he derives a conscious or unconscious comfort. But this is only another argument of the form of the arguments in the sociology of knowledge, which, however important to explaining the occurrence of a particular case, will not answer the question here at issue. To see how a resolution of Weber's difficulty can in principle be attempted, it will be useful to look at some kinds not of moral but of aesthetic argument.

Suppose that you are trying, without very much success, to persuade someone to like a painting which you yourself like very much. There may be no further consideration which you can adduce which might help to persuade him. But you will encourage him to keep on looking at it, rather than walk out of the art gallery altogether, and you will try to get him to agree, once he has looked at it a little longer, that the approbatory terms which you wish to apply to it are in fact the most appropriate. There is a remark of Kant's in the *Critique of Judgement* which goes directly to the crux of the matter: to describe something as beautiful, says Kant, is to claim that everyone ought to give his approval to it.[1] What this means is that if I am trying to persuade someone that, say, Titian's *Entombment* is a 'good' picture, I am not merely trying to persuade him, as Weldon would suggest, that I should like him to get some fun out of it too. I am trying to persuade him that words like 'good', not merely words like 'pleasurable', are those which should properly be applied to it.

The analogy may be applied to political argument. If, in what we might call a Weberian situation, there is no more factual evidence which either party would admit to be such as could alter his views, one does not simply (unless out of tedium and fatigue) 'agree to differ' and go away. One tries instead to secure the approval of one's interlocutor to the picture of the ideal society conjured up by the implementation of one's own political philosophy, and one tries to get him to accept that terms of approbation are more appropriate to one's own picture than to his. 'But surely', one says, 'it is more important that nobody willing to work should be allowed to remain unemployed than that extra entrepreneurial initiative should be rewarded by incentive payments', or whatever it may be. If he still does not agree, the best one can do is to take him again through the details of one's picture. One will try to show him as vividly as possible what it is like for people willing to work to be unemployed, and get him to agree that terms of sufficient disapprobation are appropriate to override his claim that it is more important to reward entrepreneurial initiative by the standards of commutative justice.

A further analogy may be suggested by the sort of everyday arguments which we conduct about the character of other people. The point about the choice of approbatory or disapprobatory terms can be nicely illustrated by the joke which underlies the so-called 'irregular verbs'. It is the same observed behaviour which is being described in each case, but the choice of terms depends entirely on the viewpoint of the speaker. For example: I travel, you tour, he trips; or, I am outspoken, you are tactless, he is offensive. There is no objective criterion to which appeal can be made in order to settle the most appropriate term. It is a question of persuading one's interlocutor by some other means that the crucial term that one wishes to apply is the one which ought to be chosen. 'But surely,' one says, 'given the circumstances, you can't say that *that* is cruelty', and so on.

It is also worth noting that in arguments about personal character there are the same sort of minimal standards agreed upon as in disputes between rival political philosophies. Nobody commends the character of a person on the ground that he is selfish or cruel any more than political philosophers support their recommendations on the ground that they will maximize human suffering. The problem, in either case, is to establish what overtones of approval or blame are to be applied to a situation about whose factual content there is no dispute. This is a philosophical problem, not a sociological one, and there will be no positivistic solution to it.

The point is, of course, the same as that which underlies Weber's whole position on 'value-relevance', and which derives from the fundamental difference between persons and actions on the one hand and objects and events on the other. But the fact that, as Weber saw, we are always confronted with a choice of terms, whether in sociological or philosophical discussion, need not entail the further implication that any such choice is inherently unarguable. It is this further assumption of Weber's which I am concerned to dispute. It is in fact possible to attack or defend the application of particular terms to a given case in such a way that one or other of the parties to the dispute may be induced to change his mind. Moreover, this will require an appeal both to the sociological evidence and to the philosophical presuppositions underlying the praise or blame which it is suggested that the evidence should evoke.

There is, naturally, no guarantee that one's attempt at persuasion will be successful. But it would be just as much of a mistake to suppose that the attempt can ever be known to be irretrievably foredoomed to failure. No political or aesthetic argument can be closed beyond recovery; nobody can assert as an immutable fact that he will never come to think Picasso a good painter, or abandon his belief in historical materialism and the political philosophy entailed by it. This is not only because philosophical presuppositions are insufficiently definitive (although this does not make them, as Weber would have it, unarguable). It is also true of politics because of the provisional nature of all sociological generalization. The depiction of the ideal society implied by one's own political philosophy or *Weltanschauung* depends on sociological assumptions about what such a society would look like, and any such assumptions are subject to the ineluctable limitations imposed on all generalizations or theories in social science.

This brings me to my concluding point. I have tried to show throughout these essays how the sociology and philosophy of politics are inextricably linked. But not only are they both inseparable; they are also in a specific sense interminable. There is never going to be a definitive and final philosophy, or even a logically perfect language such as was optimistically envisaged by Russell and the earlier Wittgenstein. Nor will there be a final and definitive social science such as was optimistically envisaged by Comte and (in some of his moods) by Marx. The social scientist is a part of the history from which his knowledge is constructed; every tomorrow, that knowledge may have to be revised or abandoned altogether. Likewise, the criteria of analysis and appraisal which any philosopher brings to the problems which he studies are themselves a part of the subject-matter which he is studying. Both philosophy and social science are thus in a sense parasitic activities; but it is their own as well as each other's washing that they are required to go on taking in.

The result of this for the study of politics is a necessary and irremediable tentativeness. Of course, such tentativeness can be claimed to apply to the natural sciences as well, for even their most confident and generalized statements may be seen (as by Professor Popper) to be only hypotheses which have thus far resisted disproof. But the tentativeness of the social sciences is of a further kind also, deriving from the two major difficulties which, as we have seen, the social scientist has to contend with—the uniqueness in some sense of the sequences with which he deals, and the meaningfulness of these sequences to those of whose actions they are composed. Sociological explanations of political behaviour and the choice of interpretation which they involve are no more immune to the possibility of challenge than the most transparent evaluations or prescriptions of traditional political theory. But though they may never be definitive, there is no need to regard them as arbitrary; and in this the sociology and the philosophy of politics are, contrary to Weber's conviction, in the same situation as each other. They are, moreover, rather less separable from each other than Weber and some others have tried to make them. To say that they are inseparable is not to deny that they are different; but it is to ask that they should always be seen to involve each other. Nor is there any useful sense in which one can be claimed to be more or less important than the other; it is equally important not only to continue to ask about how societies do behave, but also about how they ought to.

NOTES

PAGE 1

1 This view of the social sciences is, of course, far from original: it can, for instance, be found on p. 3 of Mosca's *The Ruling Class* (ed. Livingston). Unfortunately, however, Mosca's complaint that the term sociology 'still has no precise and sharply defined meaning' remains as true as ever, though the objection to it is more its imprecision than (as Mosca implies) its generality.

2 The different distinctions drawn between sociology and anthropology create a further terminological nuisance. The distinction is sometimes drawn in terms of subject-matter (simple societies *v.* complex ones) and sometimes in terms of method (participant observation *v.* survey techniques). But these distinctions, though perfectly valid, are largely irrelevant to the nature of sociology. The important distinctions of subject-matter are the different areas of collective behaviour, not the relative complexity of the societies where they occur; and the important distinction between methods is simply between those that are appropriate to a given problem and those that are not.

PAGE 2

1 A distinction is made by Professors Bendix and Lipset on the grounds that political science starts with the effect of the State on society, whereas political sociology starts with the effect of society on the State: see R. Bendix and S. M. Lipset, 'Political Sociology: an Essay and Bibliography', *Current Sociology*, VI (1957), 87. This is, however, a distinction impossible to apply in practice, and I cannot see why it should be useful even in theory, since the two so closely involve each other.

2 There is, however, a tripartite distinction which can be drawn between political science, political theory and political philosophy. This distinction, which derives from a very

different tradition of political thought from that underlying these essays, has been interestingly expounded by Eric Weil in an issue of the *Revue Française de Science Politique* devoted to political theory: see 'Philosophie Politique, Théorie Politique', *op. cit.* XI (1961), 267-94. Political science is, of course, demarcated by its empirical and (as far as possible) value-free content. But the further distinction between political theory and political philosophy is more intricate and subtle than I can do justice to here. Political theory, in Weil's sense, is prescriptive but also explanatory: it assumes certain basic political ends which it instructs the statesman how to pursue, but it also sets out to detect 'les forces profondes des événements de surface, les facteurs décisifs des épiphénomènes'. It involves, moreover, the Marxian emphasis on *praxis* which recurs among continental theorists (e.g. Lukacs and Sartre). Political philosophy, by contrast, is concerned rather to comprehend and to adjudicate between rival political theories. Political philosophy, unlike political theory, is not bound to a given set of historical circumstances: the great political philosophers have been, on Weil's argument, less champions of the Left or Right than interpreters at the deepest level of man and his relation to the world. Weil's distinction does not invalidate the distinction between fact and value (which is in any case a fluid one at its fringes), nor does it directly impinge on the issues which I shall for the most part be discussing about the scope of political science. I hope, however, that I have said enough in this one note to indicate its interest.

3 Psychological laws (or theories) might, of course, be of very different kinds. They might embody generalized explanations deriving from Freudian insights, or the sort of accounts of collective behaviour advanced by such post-Freudians as Erich Fromm. On the other hand, the term 'psychological' might also denote the sort of general propositions advanced by Professor Homans in his book on *Social Behaviour* (1961) where notions taken from behavioural psychology and elementary economics are used to account for aspects of small-group (and some other) behaviour. The situation is further complicated when dealing with earlier senses of

'psychology': both Weber and Durkheim are at pains to deny the dependence of sociological explanation on psychological [Weber, *The Theory of Social and Economic Organization* (transl. Parsons), p. 108; cf. *Ges. Aufs. z. Wissenschaftslehre* (2nd ed.), pp. 129, 432; Durkheim, *The Rules of Sociological Method* (ed. Catlin), pp. 101, 145], but their usage has to be taken in context. Of the two, Durkheim's doctrine of the nature of 'social facts' is the more exclusive of anything we might now understand by 'psychological' explanation.

4 Marx/Engels, *Selected Works*, II, 153.

PAGE 3

1 Examples of terms which might have an explanatory value in several different areas of collective behaviour are Durkheim's 'anomie' or the notion of 'relative deprivation' developed by American social psychologists. This may or may not apply, however, to the purely classificatory vocabulary of Talcott Parsons (on which see, for example, Homans, *op. cit.* pp. 10–11).

PAGE 4

1 Moscow English edn., p. 111.
2 *Système de Politique Positive* (1851), I, 12. (I have given a slightly more bombastic rendering than the standard Bridges translation.)

PAGE 6

1 W. Ross Ashby, *An Introduction to Cybernetics* (1956), p. 40. Cf. E. R. Leach, *Rethinking Anthropology* (1961), p. 7: 'I don't want to turn anthropology into a branch of mathematics but I believe we can learn a lot by starting to think about society in a mathematical way. Considered mathematically society is not an assemblage of things but an assemblage of variables.'
2 M. Mandelbaum, 'Societal Facts', *Brit. J. Sociol.* VI (1955), 307–9.

PAGE 8

1 R. G. Collingwood, *The Idea of History* (1946), p. 115.

Notes

PAGE 11

1 *The Theory of Social and Economic Organization*, p. 88. (This is in fact the opening section of Weber's posthumous *Wirtschaft und Gesellschaft*.)

PAGE 12

1 *Ibid.* p. 97.

PAGE 14

1 K. R. Popper, *The Open Society and its Enemies* (3rd edn., 1957), II, 292.
2 *The Poverty of Historicism* (2nd edn., 1960), p. 145, n. 1.

PAGE 16

1 Stuart Hampshire, *Thought and Action* (1959), p. 168. The same thought underlies, I think, the remark which Wittgenstein makes in the more general context of language as such (*Philosophical Investigations*, para. 122) about the notion of a 'perspicuous representation' (*übersichtliche Darstellung*). 'This notion', says Wittgenstein, 'is of fundamental significance for us. It characterizes the form of account we give, the way we look at things. (Is this a 'Weltanschauung'?)'

PAGE 17

1 It is, however, possible in principle to treat the effect of the prediction simply as an additional variable by which the prediction can be modified. This can be formally proved: see Herbert A. Simon, *Models of Man* (1957), pp. 82-3. Simon bases his proof on Brouwer's fixed-point theorem, of which he gives an intuitive demonstration (cf. R. D. Luce and H. Raiffa, *Games and Decisions* (1957), pp. 392-3), although —as he allows in his Introduction (p. 6)—such formidable mathematics are not needed for the case where a single variable only is being predicted. The fact remains, however, that (as Simon is at pains to make clear) this is a proof in principle only: if voters choose to change their minds for no better reason than to discomfit pollsters, the pollsters will not be rescued even by Brouwer's fixed-point theorem.

PAGE 18

1. Paul F. Lazarsfeld, 'The American Soldier: an Expository Review', *Publ. Opin. Quart.* XIII (1949), 380.

PAGE 27

1. Adam Ferguson, *Principles of Moral and Political Science* (Edinburgh, 1792), I, 24. I do not mean, however, to imply that Ferguson was not an author considerably ahead of his time. Marx, indeed, credited him with the first clear exposition of the ill-effects of the division of labour; but Marx always tended to be as generous in acknowledging his debts to his predecessors, if dead, as reluctant to admit the smallest influence from his contemporaries.

PAGE 30

1. *Philosophy of Right* (ed. Knox), para. 288.

PAGE 33

1. The quotation is from 'Aus der Kritik der Hegelschen Staatsrecht', in the *Marx-Engels Gesamtausgabe*, I, 1, i, 492. There is a risk of confusion of titles because of Marx's article 'Zur Kritik der Hegelschen Rechtsphilosophie' which appeared in the *Deutsch-Französische Jahrbücher* of 1844 (*Gesamtausgabe*, I, 1, i, 607–21) and in an English translation in 1926 (ed. Stenning).

PAGE 34

1. See the obituary by Carl Menger in the *Jahrbücher für Nationalökonomie und Statistik*, III, 1 (1891), 196. [I owe this reference to Kaethe Mengelberg, *J. Hist. Ideas*, XXII (1961), 268, n. 10.]
2. L. von Stein, *Geschichte der Sozialen Bewegung in Frankreich von 1789 bis auf unsere Tage* (Leipzig, 1850), pp. xxxi and xliii.
3. These two quotations are taken from passages translated in T. B. Bottomore and M. Rubel (eds.), *Karl Marx: Selected Writings in Sociology and Social Philosophy*, pp. 216 and 220.

Notes

PAGE 37

1 Émile Durkheim, *Professional Ethics and Civic Morals* (English edn., 1957), p. 43. The French edition of these lectures was first published only in 1950, in Istanbul.

PAGE 38

1 A complete definition would, of course, require a strict criterion for distinguishing public and private, which I have not attempted to give. But the difficulty of borderline cases does not demolish the validity of the distinction. Miss Arendt's discussion, in chapter II of *The Human Condition* (1958), does not offer a strict criterion either, but highlights what she considers the two significant features of the public: first, that it involves 'publicity'; and second, that it is 'common' in the sense of being 'common to all of us'. Perhaps the best that can be done is to look at the distinction in terms of social context or role: 'father' is a private role, 'citizen' or 'voter' a public one, and so on. This still leaves borderline cases, however. Sometimes these can be distinguished by such questions as 'who pays?' Here, a teacher, for instance, may be seen to be either private (tutor to a family) or public (professor at a State university). But this will only occasionally settle the matter, for people may act in a public capacity without being paid by anyone at all. What Weber calls a 'politically oriented corporate group (*Anstaltsbetrieb*)'—a body, that is, which without itself exercising power tries to affect its distribution, maintenance or transfer—may act in either or both capacities. When a voluntary organization for, say, the preservation of historic buildings gives money for the reconstruction of an interesting ruin, it is acting in a private capacity; when it lobbies Parliament for legislation in support of its aims, it is acting publicly. No hard and fast rule can be laid down. But an abundance of examples can be cited to show that the distinction is a real one.

PAGE 39

1 L. T. Hobhouse, *Social Development* (1924), pp. 50-1. I am, of course, being rather unfair to Hobhouse in extracting

from its context this one fragmentary quotation, particularly since he goes on in the same passage to emphasize precisely the political/social distinction I have been speaking of: he explicitly says (p. 51) that 'State institutions are only a fraction of the common life, and there are numerous cases in which no stretching can produce coincidence of membership'. But the fact remains that Hobhouse never does succeed in giving a satisfactory account of the State. He was concerned to distinguish the 'democratic or humanitarian' view from the metaphysical, by which he meant to emphasize the subordination of the State to the community rather than the other way round. But he neither gives a satisfactory account of the sociological determinants of the scope and limits of State action, nor an adequate philosophical criterion for the restriction of State action to the 'common good'.

PAGE 40

1 Gabriel A. Almond, 'Introduction: a Functional Approach to Comparative Politics' in Almond and James S. Coleman (eds.), *The Politics of the Developing Areas* (1960), p. 7.

PAGE 44

1 The suggestion that Lukacs's recantation may have been genuine is made by Morris Watnick in a study of Lukacs first published in *Soviet Survey* and subsequently reprinted in L. Labedz (ed.), *Revisionism* (1962), ch. x. Watnick's suggestion is that the advent of Hitlerism may have induced a strong revulsion in Lukacs against his German teachers—Dilthey, Simmel and Weber. Lukacs, although he remained loyal to Nagy after the defeat of the Hungarian rising in 1956, seems still to have been for many years a firm Stalinist, and cannot really be claimed as a champion by the liberal revisionists. Even *History and Class-Consciousness* could, despite its anti-materialism, be as well called Leninist as liberal. The book is almost unobtainable in the original (though there is a copy in the British Museum), but a French translation is now available by K. Axelos and J. Blois (Éditions de Minuit, 1960). The doctrine to which Lukacs

reverted after his recantation is that of Lenin's *Materialism and Empirio-Criticism*—the same work in which (see chapter IV, p. 66, n. 1) Lenin is rude about Sorel.

PAGE 45

1 Strictly speaking, some qualification is necessary because at several points in the early writings Marx argues against what he there means by materialism. In the critique of Hegel from which I quoted in chapter II he at one point speaks of the 'krasse Materialismus' of the Prussian bureaucracy, and in the last of his series of articles on the 'Debatten über das Holzdiebstahlgesetz' (1842) he talks about 'Dieser verworfene Materialismus'. It seems fairly clear, however, that he is here using the term in what we could call its ordinary-language use; cf. his use of 'Idealist' in an early letter to Arnold Ruge (*Marx-Engels Gesamtausgabe*, I, 1, i, 564), and in the 'Zur Kritik der Hegelschen Rechtsphilosophie' (*ibid.* p. 619)—the *locus classicus* for the 'pre-Marxist' Marx.
2 Marx to P. V. Annenkov, 28 December 1846 (*Marx/Engels Selected Correspondence*, p. 50).

PAGE 46

1 Marx did, however, continue to praise the genuine feeling and style of Proudhon's *What is Property?* despite the vehemence of his attack on *The Philosophy of Poverty*; see his letter to J. B. Schweitzer, 24 January 1865 (reprinted in *The Poverty of Philosophy*, Moscow English edn., pp. 218 ff.).
2 *Capital* (Moscow English edn.), I, 20. For the praise of Hegel there expressed by Marx, cf. his letter to L. Kugelmann, 27 June 1870 (*Selected Correspondence*, pp. 290–1).

PAGE 47

1 Émile Durkheim, *Socialism and Saint-Simon* (ed. Gouldner), p. 7.

PAGE 48

1 Alienation has also a specifically political meaning, for the State is itself an instance of objectification whereby the

community is divorced from itself. See *The German Ideology* (ed. Pascal), pp. 22-3. Eventually, of course, in Marx's basically anarchist Utopia, the State was to be reabsorbed into society (and thereby abolished altogether); but this does not diminish the importance of his analysis of the empirical distinction as he found it. I am here following up his discussion of economic and social alienation rather than his view of the State because, though less directly political, I think it gives a clearer illustration of my point.

2 *Economic and Philosophic Manuscripts of 1844* (Moscow English edn.), p. 15.

PAGE 49

1 *Ibid.* p. 27; cf. p. 71 and elsewhere.
2 *The German Ideology* (ed. Pascal), p. 22.

PAGE 51

1 Hannah Arendt, *The Human Condition* (1958), p. 91.
2 *Capital* (Moscow English edn.), I, 78.
3 *Economic and Philosophic Manuscripts of 1844*, p. 104.

PAGE 54

1 R. Aron, *Introduction to the Philosophy of History* (English edn., 1961), p. 93. Cf. F. H. Tenbruck, 'Die Genesis der Methodologie Max Webers', *Köln. Zeits. Soziol.* XI (1959), 602.
2 Karl Löwith, 'Max Weber und Karl Marx', *Archiv für Sozialwissenschaft und Sozialpolitik*, LXVII (1932), 53-99, 175-214.

PAGE 57

1 Weber gives a number of slightly different definitions of charismatic authority. I have here cited the version in *Wirtschaft und Gesellschaft* (4th edn.), p. 124 as translated in M. Rheinstein (ed.), *Max Weber on Law and Economy in Society*, p. xl. A slightly different translation is given by Parsons (*The Theory of Social and Economic Organization*, p. 328). See also Parsons, *op. cit.* pp. 358-9, H. H. Gerth and C. Wright Mills (eds.), *From Max Weber*, pp. 295-6 and *Wirtschaft und Gesellschaft*, p. 555.
2 Leo Strauss, *Natural Right and History* (1953), p. 57.
3 Gerth and Mills, *op. cit.* p. 53.

Notes

PAGE 66

1 Lenin, in a passage in *Materialism and Empirio-Criticism*, dismisses Sorel as a 'notorious muddlehead' (*Works*, XIII, 249). The context, however, is a discussion of the theories of Poincaré—a topic on which neither Lenin nor Sorel had any great competence to pronounce. Sorel's admiration for Lenin was in any case much later than his discussion of Poincaré, which occurs in his *Préoccupations Métaphysiques des Physiciens Modernes* (1907). In 1919 he added an appendix to the fourth edition of the *Reflections on Violence* in which he praised Lenin but stated explicitly that he had no reason to believe that Lenin made use of any of the ideas to be found in his writings. Sorel did perhaps have some influence on the Syndicalist movement. But, ironically enough, his theories were most successfully exemplified in Spain, where he was largely unread: though translated in 1915, the *Reflections on Violence* were disregarded except by purely literary circles and, later, the Falangists (Gerald Brenan, *The Spanish Labyrinth* (2nd edn., 1950), p. 171 and n. 2).

PAGE 67

1 *Social Contract*, Book III, chapter 4: 'If we take the term in its strict meaning, no true democracy has existed, nor ever will.'
2 *Political Parties* (1st English edn., 1915), p. 401.
3 *The Ruling Class* (ed. Livingston), p. 50.

PAGE 69

1 For the three passages quoted, see *The Mind and Society*, paras. 2031, 2254, 2057. Pareto does make clear (para. 2051) that not all the members of the governing élite at a given time need exemplify the suitable residues: they may, as aristocracies often do, survive for a time before their replacement from below. But this does not improve the formulation of his theory, since no criterion for decadence is adequately given except subsequent replacement: *entry* into the governing élite is still by sole virtue of the suitable residues.

PAGE 71

1 M. Ostrogorski, *Democracy and the Organization of Political Parties* (London, 1902), II, 608, 610.

PAGE 72

1 *Encycl. Soc. Sci.* ('Intellectuals'), VIII, 120, 'indeed it may be stated as a historical law that class movements are led by members of the classes against which they are directed...the bourgeoisie becomes the fencing master of the proletariat'.

PAGE 75

1 I am using the term 'élite' always in the sense of Pareto's 'governing élite': that is to say, an élite of power, not simply of prestige. The unqualified term does, however, normally have a wider connotation (as it does in Pareto's definition). If the decisive criterion is ability or prestige, it is clear that every society will have a plurality of élites which will not be coterminous. It can further be argued that an élite epitomizes by definition the 'ideal standards of a given culture' (S. F. Nadel, 'The Concept of Social Elites', *Int. Soc. Sci. Bull.* VIII (1956), 422). The governing élite, however, might well not fit this requirement, so that the safest usage is probably always to specify which élite is meant—governing or power élite, intellectual élite, status élite and so on. If the definition is too wide (for example, all those in positions of actual or potential *influence* in a given society), it risks proving of little value for explanation or even generalization. I use it here as synonymous with governing élite purely for convenience, since no wider sense is relevant.

2 M. Duverger, *Political Parties* (English edn., 1954), p. 425.

PAGE 76

1 J. A. Schumpeter, *Capitalism, Socialism and Democracy* (4th edn., 1954), p. 269; on democracy as the rule of the politician, pp. 284 ff.

PAGE 82

1 J. D. Stewart, *British Pressure Groups: their Role in Relation to the House of Commons* (1958), p. 244. It is noticeable that

several of the studies done of pressure-groups in Britain have been done by American political scientists; there even appeared an article in the *Virginia Quarterly Review* in 1930 by the author of *Group Representation before Congress* entitled 'Great Britain has Lobbies Too' (cited in Allen M. Potter, *Organized Groups in British National Politics* (1961), p. 13). The term 'pressure-group' seems to be of untraced origin: it is not used in A. F. Bentley's *The Process of Government: a Study of Social Pressure* (1908), but was current in the United States by the 1920's.

PAGE 83

1 R. A. Dahl, *A Preface to Democratic Theory* (1956), pp. 150, 146.
2 D. E. Butler, *The Electoral System in Britain 1918–1951* (1953), p. 1.

PAGE 89

1 My source for this is Peter H. Rossi, 'Four Landmarks in Voting Research' in E. Burdick and A. J. Brodbeck (eds.), *American Voting Behavior* (1959), n. 20 (p. 438).

PAGE 90

1 The most comprehensive critique of the voting studies to date is H. Daudt, *Floating Voters and the Floating Vote* (Leiden, 1961). In addition to pointing out ambiguities or inconsistencies in the voting studies, Daudt also suggests that more voters (and more intelligent voters) are liable to change their minds than the voting studies imply. Certainly, the consistency of the electorate can be credited as much to the consistency of the parties' broad image as to a bovine obstinacy on the part of the voter. See John Plamenatz, 'Electoral Studies and Democratic Theory', *Pol. Studies*, VI (1958), p. 8: 'The working-man who votes Labour because he believes that the Labour Party is the working-man's friend, or the landlord who votes Conservative for a similar reason, is making a sensible use of his vote. More sensible, perhaps, than if he allowed himself to be swayed by arguments for or against, say, a strong policy in the Middle East.' Thus the

most interesting voters are (as they were to Lazarsfeld) the changers. Daudt comments (p. 168) that 'no survey questionnaire has yet, as far as we know, contained the obvious question, *why* has the voting choice been changed since the previous election'. We do, however, know an increasing amount about the changers. A study of two constituencies in the British election of 1959 found that 8 per cent of their sample changed from one party to another during the campaign but that the long-term changers (between 1955 and 1959) were those decisive for the result (J. Trenaman and D. McQuail, *Television and the Political Image* (1961), pp. 207 ff.). On the national level, the Gallup poll found that 12 per cent of respondents made up their minds during the campaign, a figure which has been argued to show that 'A weakening of the tendency to vote from habit appears to be one of the effects of current social changes' (D. E. Butler and R. Rose, *The British General Election of 1959* (1960), p. 200). Even allowing, however, that the changers deserve more explanation than the rest, and even if the behaviour of the rest should not surprise political scientists or alarm political philosophers, the voting studies do still raise the broader question of whether this now well-documented behaviour may not require a reformulation of democratic theory which fits more closely to the facts.

PAGE 92

1 It is also true, of course, in the natural sciences that predicted correlations do not entail final proof or explanation. Indeed, the picture given by Professor Popper in *The Logic of Scientific Discovery* is precisely of the closest approach to proof being a succession of unsuccessful attempts at falsification. The social sciences, however, do still have a difficulty over and above this to which Humean notions of cause and effect are irrelevant, and it is this point which I am making here. It is the same point which Mill fails to see in his discussion of 'uniformities of coexistence', 'ethological laws' and so on. It is not, perhaps, quite such a failure as his antipositivist critics sometimes argue, for he is aware both that the experimental method is inapplicable to human affairs

and that empirical laws of society based on uniformities of co-existence or succession require to be supplemented by psychological laws about human nature (his 'Inverse Deductive Method'). But he still supposes that this could yield 'complete proof' (given adequate evidence) on a natural-science model, without realizing that—apart from the impossibility of 'complete proof' even in the natural sciences—his laws of human nature must be of a different logical order because of the meaningful nature of human action.

PAGE 93

1 The presuppositions of the Michigan school are set out at some length in their most recent and general work *The American Voter* by Angus Campbell *et al.* (1960). The superiority explicitly claimed by the authors for the attitudinal approach over the sociological is on the grounds (p. 17) that 'the distribution of social characteristics in a population varies but slowly over a given period of time. Yet crucial fluctuations in the national vote occur from election to election. Such fluctuation cannot be accounted for by independent variables which, over brief spans of time, do not vary. The attitudinal approach directed more attention to political objects of orientation, such as the candidates and issues, which do shift in the short term.' This, however, is to caricature the sociological explanation. There is no need to deny that issues and candidates can swing elections. But given that (as nobody would dispute) Eisenhower's personal popularity won him many votes, the question to ask is 'whose?'. The statements 'many people voted for Roosevelt because of the Depression', 'many people voted Democrat because they were relatively poor' and 'many people voted for Eisenhower because they liked him as a candidate' are all equally defensible. But an explanation of voting behaviour on a given occasion requires statements of all three types: a historical explanation showing which party stood for which obvious interest, a sociological explanation showing what sort of people deviated from their obvious interest, and a psychological explanation showing what sort of

'deviants' a particular candidate or issue appealed to. The social characteristics against which voters are analysed are not claimed by anyone to provide the complete explanation by themselves. But to discover how many people voted for Eisenhower because they liked him is only a description of his effect on the election; it is not an explanation of his effect until we know more about the people so affected. The Michigan authors claim that their 'field theoretical' approach has the advantage of 'maximizing explanatory power in the early stages of enquiry' (p. 35). My disagreement with this question-begging use of 'explanatory' will, I hope, be clear from the discussion in the text. I should, however, emphasize that *The American Voter* contains a great deal of useful material on more fundamental influences on voting behaviour than purely 'attitudinal' differences.

PAGE 95

1 André Siegfried, *Tableau politique de la France de l'Ouest sous la troisième république* (1913), ch. XII. In discussing the Breton fishermen, however, Siegfried points out a big difference between the 'marins propriétaires' and the 'pêcheurs non-propriétaires'. In the case of the latter, he lists a number of factors both in their market-situation and in their work-situation likely to predispose them to radicalism. His method, of course, is not the sample survey but the sometimes misleading technique now known as 'ecological correlation'—relating collective attributes of a region or district to each other. For some of the evidence on the radicalism of different occupations, see S. M. Lipset, *Political Man* (1960), ch. VII.

PAGE 103

1 William Kornhauser, *The Politics of Mass Society* (1959), p. 223. See also the relevant sections of Lipset, *op. cit.*

PAGE 105

1 Colin Leys, 'Models, Theories and the Theory of Political Parties', *Pol. Studies*, VII (1959), 127.

Notes

PAGE 107

1 Anthony Downs, *An Economic Theory of Democracy* (1957), p. 297 (Propositions 2 and 3).

PAGE 111

1 This quotation is taken from Malinowski's article 'Anthropology' in the *Encyclopaedia Britannica* (1926), Suppl. vol. I, 132.
2 A. R. Radcliffe-Brown, *Structure and Function in Primitive Society* (1952), p. 145.
3 *Ibid.* p. 180.
4 See George C. Homans, *The Human Group* (1950), p. 271; Homans and David M. Schneider, *Marriage, Authority and Final Causes* (1955), p. 16.

PAGE 112

1 Durkheim, *The Rules of Sociological Method* (ed. Catlin), p. 90.

PAGE 113

1 See Ernest Nagel, *Logic Without Metaphysics* (1956), part I, chapter 10, 'A Formalization of Functionalism'.
2 Carl G. Hempel, 'The Logic of Functional Analysis' in L. Gross (ed.), *Symposium on Sociological Theory* (1959), pp. 301–2.

PAGE 114

1 Kingsley Davis, 'The Myth of Functional Analysis in Sociology and Anthropology', *Amer. Sociol. Rev.* XXIV (1959), pp. 757–72.

PAGE 116

1 S. F. Nadel, *Foundations of Social Anthropology* (1951), p. 368.
2 Homans and Schneider, *op. cit.*, on Claude Lévi-Strauss, *Les Structures Elémentaires de la Parenté* (1949).

PAGE 117

1 P. M. Blau, *The Dynamics of Bureaucracy* (1955), p. 8.
2 Neil J. Smelser, *Social Change in the Industrial Revolution* (1959), p. 22.

PAGE 118

1   Nadel, *op. cit.* p. 378.
2   R. K. Merton, *Social Theory and Social Structure* (rev. edn., 1957), p. 73.

PAGE 120

1   Talcott Parsons, '*Voting* and the Equilibrium of the American Political System', in E. Burdick and A. J. Brodbeck (eds.), *American Voting Behaviour* (1959), p. 115 and n. 48.
2   *Ibid.* p. 114.

PAGE 121

1   David Lockwood, 'Some Remarks on "The Social System"', *Brit. J. Sociol.* VII (1956), 136. Parsons is, in fact, quite explicit about his assumption that 'the stabilization of the processes of mutual interaction within complementary roles is a fundamental tendency of interaction', but seems not to realize how far the question is begged by the use of 'fundamental'.

PAGE 123

1   This use of the term 'function' is demonstrated in S. I. Benn and R. S. Peters, *Social Principles and the Democratic State* (1959), p. 240. The sense which is given to the general will by interpreting it as a functional concept is not, of course, the only possible one, but it does, as Benn and Peters show, make better sense of Bosanquet's version. The distinction between a person's 'actual' and 'real' will in Bosanquet's sense is then that between his personal objectives and the institutional duties deriving from his role in the total system of functionally related roles and institutions which constitute a society.

PAGE 126

1   Patricia F. Kendall and P. F. Lazarsfeld, 'Problems of Survey Analysis', in Merton and Lazarsfeld (eds.), *Continuities in Social Research* (1950), p. 158, n. 26. Cf. Lazarsfeld, 'Interpretation of Statistical Relations as a Research Operation', in Lazarsfeld and Morris Rosenberg (eds.), *The Language of Social Research* (1955), p. 125: 'If we have a

relationship between "x" and "y"; and if for any *antecedent* test factor the partial relationships between "x" and "y" do not disappear, then the original relationship should be called a causal one.'

PAGE 127

1 Herbert A. Simon, 'Spurious Correlation: a Causal Interpretation' in *Models of Man* (1957), p. 41.

PAGE 128

1 Hanan C. Selvin, 'A Critique of Tests of Significance in Survey Research', *Amer. Sociol. Rev.* XXII (1957), 519–27.

PAGE 131

1 The application of factor analysis to political attitudes in an immediately topical context is illustrated by J. Trenaman and D. McQuail, *Television and the Political Image* (1961). Their conclusion is that 'of the great mass of opinions which make up political images, about two-thirds can be resolved into three or four general tendencies' (p. 28). The technique, however, statistically elegant and powerful though it is, turns out in this as in many other cases to be oddly disappointing. That a factor which can be interpreted as 'the betterment of the common people' accounts for a goodish part of the Labour Party image hardly needs to be demonstrated by so much effort; and the communalities shown in the tables (pp. 274–9) are not so remarkable as to seem to justify the use of what may be an over-refined tool for analysis of this kind. Its use should, perhaps, be regarded chiefly as exploratory, and to be justified by its application in contexts where cruder presuppositions are thereby shown to be incorrect.

PAGE 137

1 *From Max Weber*, ed. Gerth and Mills, p. 181.
2 *Ibid.* pp. 186–7. (I have altered 'honour' to 'prestige' for *Ehre*.)

PAGE 139

1 T. H. Marshall, *Citizenship and Social Class* (1950), p. 92.

2 Two further examples may be worth appending from books recently written. The first is from a widely praised American textbook, Harry M. Johnson's *Sociology: a Systematic Introduction* (1960), where a social class is defined (p. 469) as 'a more or less endogamous stratum consisting of families of about equal prestige who are or would be acceptable to one another for "social" interaction that is culturally regarded as more or less symbolic of equality'. This, clearly, is a reasonable and potentially useful definition of (in Weberian terms) a status-stratum. Johnson is, of course, perfectly entitled to regard stratification by status as the most important or even the only dimension of social stratification, but to suggest that his is merely a different conception of 'class' from the Marxian (pp. 504-6) is misleading. It is a disagreement of substance, and to see it as a disagreement of definition of the same term 'class' creates a confusion which could be easily avoided by using Weber's terms both for Marxian theory and for Johnson's views on status. The second example is from Ralf Dahrendorf's *Class and Class Conflict in an Industrial Society* (English edn., 1959), where in terms of the model suggested 'the term "class" signifies conflict groups that are generated by the differential distribution of authority in imperatively coordinated associations' (p. 204). This, in Weberian terms, amounts to the (cogent) suggestion that stratification by the third dimension, power, is more important in prosperous industrialized societies than stratification by economic class, particularly from the point of view of the generation of social conflict. Once again, it would surely lessen the chance of confusion to state this as a disagreement of substance with previous theorists of class, expressed in a standard terminology, rather than to put it forward in the form of yet another definition of the term 'class'.

PAGE 140

1 *The Eighteenth Brumaire of Louis Bonaparte* (International Publishers edn., New York), p. 109.

PAGE 141

1 David Lockwood, *The Blackcoated Worker* (1958), p. 15. Cf. pp. 202, 205-8.

Notes

PAGE 143

1 David Lockwood, 'The New Working Class', *Arch. Eur. Sociol.* I (1960), 253. For an American discussion, cf. B. Berger, *Working-Class Suburb* (1960), pp. 91–8.

PAGE 147

1 M. Fortes, 'The Political System of the Tallensi of the Northern Territories of the Gold Coast', in Fortes and E. E. Evans-Pritchard (eds.), *African Political Systems* (1940), p. 250.

PAGE 148

1 Robert C. Tucker, 'Towards a Comparative Politics of Movement-Régimes', *Amer. Pol. Sci. Rev.* LV (1961), 282.
2 J. L. Talmon, *The Origins of Totalitarian Democracy* (1952), pp. 6–7. Cf. H. Marcuse, *Reason and Revolution* (1954), pp. 180–1, 'There is no concept less compatible with Fascist ideology than that which founds the state on a universal and rational law that safeguards the interests of every individual, whatever the contingencies of his natural and social status'.

PAGE 150

1 S. M. Lipset, *Political Man* (1960), ch. v.

PAGE 156

1 'Science as a Vocation' ('*Wissenschaft als Beruf*'), in Gerth and Mills (eds.), *From Max Weber*, p. 143. The speech was first published in 1919. I give the German title because of the misleading overtones of 'science' as a translation of *Wissenschaft*. Weber is not talking about what would be meant in an English address of this title by 'science' (that is, natural science) but by what could perhaps be better rendered 'academic research'.

PAGE 157

1 In *The Methodology of the Social Sciences* (ed. Shils), pp. 1–47, esp. pp. 20–5.

PAGE 164
1 G. Lukacs, *Geschichte und Klassenbewusstsein* (1923), p. 243.
2 K. Mannheim, *Ideology and Utopia* (1936), p. 137.

PAGE 165
1 R. K. Merton, *Social Theory and Social Structure* (rev. edn., 1957), p. 507.
2 These two prerequisites of science as we understand it are explicitly emphasized by Weber in the speech already referred to (Gerth and Mills, pp. 141-2), though the statement as made should strictly speaking be qualified. Weber points out that 'In India one finds the beginning of a logic quite similar to that of Aristotle'; and the experimental method was not totally unknown to the Greeks (Ptolemy, for instance, devised several optical experiments). But the point which Weber lays stress on is that the *significance* of the concept and the experiment were only realized at these particular places and times.

PAGE 167
1 Lukacs, *op. cit.* p. 232. *Unbefangenheit* is rendered in the French translation as 'largeur de vue', which seems to me to be questionable; but it is certainly true that Lukacs is using the word in a more loaded sense than would normally by understood by 'freedom from prejudice'. To Lukacs, the *Unbefangenheit* of Smith and Ricardo derives from their historical situation, in which their doctrines were in harmony with the interests of the ascendant class and with their own confidence in those interests. For the rather special sense of objectivity which this implies, see for instance Sartre's *Critique de la Raison Dialectique* (1960), p. 74, n. 1: 'la philosophie de Condillac, dans son siècle, dans le courant qui portrait la bourgeoisie vers la révolution et le libéralisme, était beaucoup plus vraie — comme facteur réelle de l'évolution historique — que la philosophie de Jaspers ne l'est aujourd'hui.' Neither Lukacs nor Sartre recognize Weber's distinction between a basic evaluative viewpoint and a lack of scientific objectivity; nor, for that matter, do some

other commentators on Smith and Ricardo, notably Myrdal (on whose discussion see W. Stark, *The Sociology of Knowledge* (1956), pp. 55 ff.).

PAGE 169

1 H. L. A. Hart, *The Concept of Law* (1961), p. 195.

PAGE 171

1 *Critique of Judgement* (transl. Bernard), p. 92.

INDEX

Page numbers in italic type indicate references to notes

Al Ghazali, 153-4
alienation, 47 ff., 55, *183-4*
Almond, G., 40, *182*
Althusius, 27
anarchism, 28-9, 149
anticipatory socialization, 144
Aquinas, 27
Arendt, Hannah, 37, 51, 147, *184*
Aristotle, 22, 25, 27, 37, 134, 152
Aron, R., 54, *184*
Arrow, K. J., 133
Ashby, W. Ross, *178*

Babeuf, G., 149, 170
Bagehot, W., 23, 97
Bendix, R., *176*
Benn, S. I., *192*
Bentham, 22, 42, 83, 153
Bentley, A. F., *187*
Berger, B., *195*
Blau, P. M., *191*
Bodin, 26
Bosanquet, B., *192*
Bottomore, T. B., *180*
Brenan, G., *185*
Brouwer's fixed-point theorem, *179*
Bryce, Lord, 97
Burke, 153
Butler, D. E., 83, *187*, *188*

Cabet, E., 46, 72
Campbell, A., *189*
charisma, 56-63, 69, *184*
Coleman, J. S., 40, *182*
Collingwood, R. G., *178*
Comte, A., 4, 27, 30, 31, 37, 39, 154, 162, 174
Condillac, *196*
cybernetics, 6, 114

Dahl, R., 83, *187*
Dahrendorf, R., *194*
Darwin, 2, 5, 45
Daudt, H., *187-8*
Davis, K., *191*
Dilthey, W., *182*
Downs, A., *191*
Durkheim, 7, 30, 36-8, 39, 47, 102, 112, 153, 165, *178*, *181*, *183*, *191*
Duverger, M., 75, 78, 104 ff., *186*

Engels, 2, 4, 9, 27, 28, 43 ff., 149

factor analysis, 131, *193*
Ferguson, A., 27, *180*
Feuerbach, L., 31, 47
Figgis, J. N., 24-5
Fortes, M., 146, *195*
Fourier, C., 28, 46, 72, 149
Freud, Freudianism, 12-13, 161, *177*
Fromm, E., 102, *177*
functionalism, 3, 39-41, 110 ff.

Gemeinschaft, 152-4
Gerson, 24
Gerth, H. H., *184*
Gesellschaft, 152-4
Godwin, W., 28, 29, 149
Gresham's law, 12
Grotius, 24, 27

Halévy, E., 104
Hampshire, S., 16, 52, *179*
Hart, H. L. A., 169, *197*
Hegel, 29-33, 36, 39, 41, 46, 47, *183*
Hempel, C. G., *191*
historicism, 14, 27
Hitler, 44, 77, 148, 150-1; *see also* Nazism
Hobbes, 26, 42
Hobhouse, L. T., 39-40, *181-2*

Index

Homans, G. C., 177, 178, 191
Hume, 157, 188

Jaspers, K., 196
Johnson, H. M., 194

Kant, 171
Kendall, Patricia F., 125, 192
Keynes, J. M., 166
Kierkegaard, 31
Kornhauser, W., 102, 190

Labedz, L., 182
Lazarsfeld, P. F., 18–19, 89–90, 93, 94, 119, 124–6, 180, 192–3
Leach, E. R., 178
Lenin, 28, 43, 149, 183, 185
Lévi-Strauss, C., 116, 191
Leys, C., 190
Lipset, S. M., 150–1, 176, 190, 195
Lockwood, D., 121, 141, 143, 144, 192, 194, 195
Löwith, K., 54–5, 184
Luce, R. D., 179
Lukacs, G., 44, 72, 162–4, 165, 167, 177, 182, 196
Luther, 25

Machiavelli, 25, 67, 68, 166
McQuail, D., 188, 193
Madison, J., 97
Malinowski, B., 30, 110–12, 191
Mandelbaum, M., 178
Mannheim, K., 162, 164–5, 196
Marcuse, H., 195
Marshall, A., 166
Marshall, T. H., 139, 193
Marx, 2–3, 4, 8, 22, 25 ff., 32–4, 41, 43–52, 53 ff., 64, 73–4, 102, 104, 123, 136, 139–40, 149, 153–4, 174, 178, 180, 183, 184
Marxism, 109, 113, 121–2, 161, 162 ff.
Mengelberg, Kaethe, 180
Menger, C., 180
Merton, R. K., 118–19, 120, 165, 192, 196

Michels, R., 23, 64 ff., 70 ff., 78, 79, 83, 84, 97, 142
'Michigan school', 93 ff., 189–90
Mill, J. S., 17, 23, 31, 32, 83, 96, 97, 188–9
Mill, James, 83
Mills, C. W., 184
Montesquieu, 26, 36
Morris, W., 102, 153
Mosca, G., 64, 65, 67–8, 70 ff., 83, 84, 176
Mussolini, 66, 151
Myrdal, G., 197

Nadel, S. F., 118, 186, 191, 192
Nagel, E., 191
natural law, 26, 169, 170
Nazism, 99, 101, 150–1

Ostrogorski, M., 23, 71, 88–9, 97, 186
Owen, R., 28, 149

Paine, T., 28, 149
Pareto, V., 64 ff., 68–9, 70 ff., 83, 84, 185, 186
Parsons, T., 117, 119–21, 178, 184, 192
Peron, 99, 150–1
Peters, R. S., 192
Petty, Sir W., 23
Plamenatz, J., 181
Plato, 152, 153
Plekhanov, G., 9–10
Poincaré, H., 185
Polybius, 78
Popper, K., 13–14, 17, 127, 175, 179, 188
Potter, A. M., 187
power, 79–80, 137, 145
pressure-groups, 82–6
Proudhon, P-J., 23, 29, 31, 45, 46, 149, 183

Quételet, A., 24

Radcliffe-Brown, A., 110–11, 191
Raiffa, H., 179

Rheinstein, M., *184*
Ricardo, D., 166, 167, *196–7*
Roman Catholicism, 161
Rose, R., *188*
Rossi, P. H., *187*
Rousseau, 27, 36, 46, 67, 68, 82
Rubel, M., *180*
Russell, B., 174

Saint-Simon, Henri Comte de, 27–8, 29, 36, 149, 154, 162
Sartre, J.-P., 31, *177*, *196*
Schapera, I., 36
Scheler, M., 165
Schmoller, G., 170
Schneider, D. M., *191*
Schumpeter, J. A., 76–7, 82, 87, 97, *186*
Selvin, H. C., 128–9, *193*
Siegfried, A., 95–6, *190*
significance tests, 128–31
Simmel, G., *182*
Simon, H. A., *179*, *193*
Smelser, N. J., *191*
Smith, Adam, 166, 167, *196–7*
sociology of knowledge, 47, 162 ff.
Sorel, G., 64, 65–6, 70, 73, *183*, *185*
Spencer, H., 17
Stalin, 44, 81, 99, 148, 153
Stark, W., *197*
Stein, L. von, 30, 31, 33–4, *180*

Stewart, J. D., 82, *186*
Stirner, M., 31
Strauss, L., *184*

Tallensi, 146–7, 152
Talmon, J. L., 148–9, *195*
Tenbruck, F. H., *184*
theory of games, 132–3
Tocqueville, A. de, 23, 29, 97, 102, 103
Tolstoy, 151, 156
Tönnies, F., 151–2
Trenaman, J., *188*, *193*
Troeltsch, E., 7
Tucker, R. C., *195*

uncertainty principle, 126–7

Verstehen, 11–12

Wallas, G., 89, 94
Watnick, M., *182*
Weber, 6 ff., 23, 34–8, 41, 43, 44, 52–63, 64, 69, 123, 132, 136 ff., 142, 146, 153–4, 156 ff., 166 ff., *178*, *179*, *181*, *182*, *184*, *194*, *195*, *196*
Weil, E., *177*
Weldon, T. D., 156, 157, 159, 171
welfare economics, 85
Wittgenstein, L., 174, *179*